Coaching

C   S

Coaching Champions

The Privilege
of Mentoring

by

Jess Gibson

New Leaf Press

First Edition
October 1994

ISBN: 0-89221-257-8
Library of Congress: 93-87254

Scripture quotations are from the New King James
Version unless otherwise noted.

Dedication

To my wife, Paula,
Who is a Champion
of encouragement
and hope to me, our family,
and scores of
others!

To my "Champion" children
Kim, Trace, Michael, and Jef
and their Champion spouses,
Rusty, Tammy, and Margie.

And to my "Champions" in the making, my
grandkids: Kelly, David, Jesse, Christopher,
Taryn, Tyler, Halley, Kelsey,
Ryan, and Sophia.

My children:
Pursue the Master Mentor —
His wisdom,
His understanding,
His knowledge,
And you will always be
All you can be . . .
Kingdom Champions!

Acknowledgment

Special thanks to my ever-faithful secretary Carole Clemmons, for her tireless energy getting this project ready for the editor;

To my friends, Kenny and Donna Stewart, Amway Crown-Directs, for their continued example of championship achievement;

To my mentors, past and present: my dad and mom; Mike Murdock, evangelist; Bob Harrison, Harrison International Ministries; Big Ed (wherever you are); Dick R. (my challenger); Jay Payton (my brother-in-law), who always said I could; and Dr. Lester Sumrall (the Kingdom Legend), and too many more to mention!

Contents

Preface

Are You Ready to Fly? 11

Part One: Mentors: Dealers in Hope

1. People Planters 17
2. Molding Square Bamboo 27
3. Wants, Needs, and the Big Five 37

Part Two: Coaching Your Own Champions

4. Dad and Mom as Mentors 49
5. Tender/Tough Mentoring............................ 59
6. The Family Mentoring Session 69
7. If Not You — Who? 77

Part Three: Kingdom Mentoring

8. The Ninth Wave 87
9. Hands and Hearts 95
10. Worthy of Duplication? 105
11. Identifying True Leaders 113
12. Setting the Standard 123

Part Four: Mentoring in the Marketplace

13. Buying into Another's Dream 135
14. Your Job Has No Future 145
15. Motivation and the Mentor....................... 155
16. Now It's Your Turn................................... 165

Are You Ready to Fly?

"Are you sure I'm ready?" I asked.

"As ready as you'll ever be. Go for it."

With that reassuring reply, my instructor climbed out of the airplane, waved a white handkerchief after pretending to wipe his eyes of tears, then with mock sadness said, "I'll miss you."

I chuckled, but here I was, all alone, expected to fly that little Cessna 150 into the wild, blue yonder.

As I sat there at the end of the runway, with the sound of the engine roaring in the cockpit, all I could really hear was my heart pounding louder and louder.

My lips were dry. My palms were sweaty. The adrenaline was pumping.

I was ready.

How did I know? Because I had been mentored in the fine art of flying. I knew I was really ready.

First, I had attended intensive ground school classes learning how to read charts, understand dashboard gauges, and interpret cloud formations. That was followed by airport coffee shop time with my instructor as he encouraged me, enlightened me, and critiqued my best efforts.

More flying time followed. More coffee shop time.

Then one day up in the air, my instructor looked over at me and said, "Stop at the end of the runway after the next landing, and I'll get out."

Whew! Did he really mean it?

His and my mentoring process had begun the day I first met him.

Although 30 years have passed, I can still hear his words on the day of my very first lesson: "Here's how you'll learn to fly. First, I'll do it, and you watch. Next step, we do it together. Then, you do it, and I'll watch. Finally, I'll let you go by yourself."

That, in essence, is the mentoring process:

> I do it, you watch; then
> We do it together; then
> You do it, I watch; then
> You do it alone.

Mentoring has become a buzzword in just about every field and discipline over the past few years. It's difficult not to read about "my favorite mentor" in virtually every business publication you pick up.

Everywhere we look, more emphasis is placed on the mentoring approach to business and professional development.

Why?

Because it works!

People are being planted, watered, grown, and nurtured into children of character, champions for Christ, and fruitful employees because of this age-old system of assisting others to achieve the potential that is within them.

One-third of America's major firms, including Colgate, Johnson & Johnson, AT&T, and Pacific Bell, have mentoring programs in which executives guide and counsel younger employees who show promise.

What is mentoring and how does it relate to you? In the chapters to follow you'll learn how mentoring works and how it can affect your relationships in the home, in the kingdom of God, and in the marketplace.

Oh, by the way — my first solo flight?

I made it!

I made three beautiful landings and takeoffs in that little Cessna — every bounce of them!

That began my love affair with airplanes and flying that has spanned nearly 30 years.

Today, I still love flying, but I have another fascination. I have found something better that lifts my spirits even higher than any Beechcraft or antique Stearman or classic Sopwith.

I have learned the extraordinary rewards of helping people through *mentoring*.

Part 1

Mentors: Dealers in Hope

Chapter One

People Planters

An old Chinese proverb says:

> If you're planting for a year, plant grain;
> If you're planting for a decade, plant trees;
> If you're planting for a century, plant *people.*

Mentors are people planters. They have a heart to see people grow under their mentorship.

The term comes from the Greek mythological figure Mentor, the trusted slave of Ulysses, the king of the Ithacans who was the hero of Homer's classics *The Iliad* and *The Odyssey.*

Before leaving for the Trojan War, Ulysses entrusted the care of the royal household to Mentor. Back then, it was often a custom for a nobleman to commit the rearing of his son to a wise and trusted slave. So, Ulysses gave Mentor the job of tutoring and training young Prince Telemachus.

This responsibility turned into more than either of them anticipated when Ulysses stayed away more than 20 years.

Mentor had accepted the two-decade task of developing the boy's character and trained him into manhood so that he was capable of assuming the throne if Ulysses never returned.

Today, because of the example of the mythical Mentor, a "mentor" is a coach, a teacher, a trusted counselor, a guide.

A mentor is a role model — usually someone wiser than you, someone with experience in your field, someone dedicated to helping you achieve your ambitions.

A mentor is a person who recognizes the difference between leadership and the mentoring process. They're aware of the difference between what they do and what a teacher does.

Let me explain.

A teacher imparts knowledge, instruction, and skills; a leader imparts guidance and motivation. A mentor, however, does everything a leader does, everything a teacher does, and much more.

A mentor imparts his life into the development of his protégé or "mentoree."

One on One

Tom Fleming never laid eyes on his dad, saw his

mother only twice as a boy, and was raised by grand-parents in a house they shared with 14 other people.

At 16, Tom dropped out of high school without learning to read and did time in a reform school. He lied about his age to enlist in the National Guard, and later joined the regular army where he did a stint in France.

While Tom was overseas, he suddenly felt very alone and frightened. He recalls, "My mom told me, 'When you feel down, read the Bible.' "

Good idea, except Tom couldn't read or write.

While Tom was in the service he met David, an-other soldier, who talked with him about being born again. Tom gave his heart to Christ in 1954, as David and he prayed together on the barracks floor.

A change began to take place in Tom's life. He wanted an education and decided to go to night school so he could learn to read the Bible.

In the years to come, Tom earned a high school equivalency diploma, a bachelor's degree in religious education, and a master of arts degree in regular and special education.

From there he was sent to a detention center — not as a detainee, but as a teacher for youngsters 12 to 16 who are confined while their cases move through the court system.

Today, Tom's "students" have been arrested for anything from shoplifting to sexual assault. He sees his past in the lives of his students, but the mentor in him doesn't stop there. He offers them a future. He goes on to describe himself as a "special-ed kid who is now a special-ed teacher."

The reason we include Tom Fleming in a book on mentoring is because Tom was named National Teacher of the Year in 1993, and he has a mentoring approach to teaching his unusual students.

His teaching-mentoring style is intense and personal — one on one. He says he offers his students hope by telling them they are worth something, that they can learn, and that they can change and achieve better things in life.

Tom imparts not just skill and knowledge, he pours his character, his principles, and his being into the lives of his students.

In each one of these kids he sees the seed of something greater than they are. His philosophy is expressed this way:

You can always cut open the apple and find out how many seeds are inside, but there's no way you can cut the seed and find out how many apples are in it.

As teacher/mentor, Tom challenges educators to a fresh vision and renewal. He reminds them a caring teacher can build trust and awaken the kind of hope that leads a young person to want to grow strong in mind and heart.

Tom Fleming is a tribute to the mentor/educator. Thank God for people like Tom Fleming who have a real heart to touch the lives of others.

Everybody Gets a Standing Ovation!

Jon was born with Down's Syndrome.

When his natural parents were told their son was handicapped, they refused to take him home. He was institutionalized for a while, then passed from foster home to foster home.

Nobody wanted him. He was not taught the skills other kids were taught. He wasn't even potty-trained. He was a child alone. By the age of four Jon could neither talk nor eat.

Then Jon was adopted by a loving, caring family who gave him the things he needed most: significance born out of love, hope, and a chance to grow.

Jon is one of the kids whose life has been changed as a result of the Special Olympics.

The Special Olympics has become the fastest-growing sports program in the world since it was founded by Eunice Kennedy Shriver. Nearly a million and a half handicapped athletes from every state and over 50 foreign countries compete at separate sports events every summer.

This nine year old went out on a Saturday afternoon and competed in the standing long jump and the 50-meter dash. Remember, just five years before, Jon couldn't talk or eat; he was an unhappy little boy whom life had cruelly passed by.

This warm Saturday afternoon Jon became a winner. He won two second place medals and went home clutching his ribbons in triumph.

Jon's adoptive dad said, "This is the biggest day of his life. Special Olympics is Jon's chance to be normal, to be praised. No matter whether he places first or last, everybody gets a standing ovation, a ribbon, and an opportunity to be the center of attention.

"It's absolutely astonishing, the difference it makes. You want to cry when you see the look of triumph on their faces, these kids who have so little chance to triumph."

Jon was a child who conquered. A Special Olympian! A champion.

The concept of Special Olympics is rooted in mentoring. The coaches, parents, friends, and fans all recognize that these handicapped athletes have the same desires in life that all of us have.

Three Basic Wants

If we understand the three basic wants that people have in life, we'll begin to have a better understanding of how important a mentoring relationship can be.

Want number one: Significance.

People want to make a difference. They want their achievements to be recognized. They don't want to be a face in the crowd and be swept up in the masses of mediocrity.

Children and adults want to feel important. They want to be successful in what they do and be recognized for it.

People are looking for significance and for recognition in their work. They want to be a part of the team. They want to be included.

Mentoring is an effective way to make our children, our co-workers, and our brothers and sisters in Christ feel more appreciated and to become more significant.

Number 2: Everyone is seeking hope.

Too many people today are living in hopelessly desperate situations. They are looking for hope. Everybody wants assurance in their life. They need to have faith that everything is going to turn out all right.

Hope comes from significant, meaningful relationships. We can bring hope into a person's life by mentoring them.

Napoleon once said that mentors are dealers in hope. That's what we're here to do as a mentor — to instill hope and to bring faith in the future into the lives of people who have none.

Number 3: Personal growth.

People want to experience personal progress in life. We as mentors can help them attain those personal goals.

Most of us like doing a good job and enjoy being rewarded for it. We like working in an environment where reward and recognition are assured instead of anonymity. We like having our hard work recognized by others.

Follow Me

Let's take a look at a basic truth regarding the mentoring subject. The process is as old as the Bible, so let's begin there to grasp the concept and what it can mean to us.

First of all, mentoring is spending more time with fewer people.

Jesus called 12 businessmen to follow Him. He said: "Follow Me, and I'll make you fishers of men."

Get the idea? "Follow me and I'll make [mentor] you."

Jesus' ultimate goal as a Kingdom mentor was to mentor the 12, so that when He wasn't around anymore, they would carry on His work by mentoring others to carry on their work! That's mentoring.

He said, in essence, "Come live with Me, walk with Me, listen to Me, watch Me, and you'll learn from Me. Do as I do. Be as I am." That's the making of a champion.

Please note that Jesus also met the needs of the "many" — the multitude. He fed the 5,000 and the 4,000. He healed "all" who had sickness, but He mentored only a few.

It's no different for us. We can't mentor 5,000. I can lead 5,000. I can teach a multitude, but I can only impart my life as a mentor to a few.

After surviving a nightmarish 1992 Summer Olympics, some people might have encouraged gymnast Kim Zmeskal to walk away from competing all together.

Some might. Not her mentor, Bela Karolyi.

Kim was the 1991 world champion but finished tenth all-around in the Barcelona Games and never contended for individual medals.

After the games, Zmeskal returned to Houston to finish high school and had not competed since that time. However, she continued to work out every day with the same zeal of an Olympian.

Recently, she asked Karolyi to mentor her into a

full-scale come-back at the age of 18. She has a dream
to make the '96 Olympic team.

Her mentor/coach says this about her chances.
"She is not a child anymore. She knows adversity. In
my 30 years of coaching there has never been anyone
more loyal to me than Kim."

Kim Zmeskal realizes she needed more than just a
coach. She needed a mentor to be a champion.

How about you? Do you need a mentor? Or maybe
you have the skills, experience, and desire to mentor
someone else.

Chapter Two

Molding Square Bamboo

The basis for effective mentoring is found in relationships. The relationship between the mentor and his
student is the key that causes the process to be effective.

Through a meaningful relationship, the mentor
imparts values, skills, and character.

John MacArthur Jr. illustrates this concept when
he says:

Being discipled . . . isn't accomplished
in a 10-week class; it is accomplished by

spending time with a godly individual — walking with him, feeling his heartbeat, hearing him speak, and seeing him pray.

This is mentoring. Spending time together. Walking and talking together. It is a heart-to-heart relationship where two people come together ready to pay the price that the relationship demands.

The mentoree is willing to allow the mentor access to his life to assist him in change. The mentor can be one of life's greatest tormentors as they challenge, correct, and motivate.

Square Bamboo

In his book *Heroes of Honor*, Robert Bauman, veteran missionary to Japan, tells us that more than 80 species of bamboo grow in that country. Most are inexpensive and used for construction or basic tools. But the most striking type of bamboo, called "square bamboo," is highly prized and expensive.

Bamboo naturally is round. However, a farmer who wishes to produce high-quality square bamboo will choose young stalks of the plant and clamp two "L" shaped pieces of wood tightly around the young stalk.

The stalk presses into the square as it grows; it has nowhere else to expand as it sprouts to its full height. In the square mold the bamboo experiences a painful limitation of what it would naturally be.

In addition, to give the surface of the

bamboo an unusual, irregular design, the farmer mixes acid and mud and places the mixture inside the mold before clamping it around the bamboo. If that suffering bamboo could talk, how bitterly it would complain about the farmer's method as it compares itself to the free-growing bamboo around it.

But when the process has finished and all the bamboo is cut down, the normal, free-growing round bamboo poles are bundled and thrown into trucks. They will be used, but not in important ways.

However, the square bamboo receives careful treatment, for it has become the most precious and valuable of all bamboo. It has turned into a beautiful surprise.

God may be working in your life right now, and the process seems to be unnatural and painful. But God, the God of surprises, is creating something ultimately beautiful and precious in your life. Trust Him with the outcome.[1]

God does not create great leaders. He makes great servants — who become great leaders.

Frequently the mentoring process seems unnatural and painful for the mentoree. But yielding to the mentoring process can produce something beautiful and ultimately precious in the life of the one being mentored.

The "Mentoree" Attitude

The person being mentored also assumes certain responsibilities. Whether he is a child, a weathered Christian, a new believer in Christ, or a job trainee, he or she must bring certain attitudes into the relationship if the desired results are to be attained.

- The mentoree must be eager to grow and change.
- He must be teachable.
- He must purpose to apply the things he receives from his mentor.
- He must maintain a high level of commitment to the relationship.
- He must be loyal to his mentor and the relationship.
- He must show respect to his mentor.
- He must come into the relationship with a willingness to be accountable.

I recently read a sports story about a young college basketball player who came off the bench to score 14 points in her first college game. She had 11 rebounds!

How did she do it?

She told the sports writer, "The coach told me what I had to do, and I did it."

That's the bottom line mentoree's attitude in a mentoring relationship. *"My mentor told me what I needed to do, so I did it."*

This potential champion didn't debate whether or not her team needed her to do it or not. She did not ponder the point spread nor the effect her hustling might have on the morale of the rest of the team.

No, her mentor said, "Do it."

So, she did. She achieved because she was teachable, committed, respectful, accountable, and a *doer.*

**Your associations today will determine
who you are tomorrow.**

The Mentor/Mentoree Relationship

Let's consider the following principles to shed further light into the concept of mentoring and the function of the mentor/mentoree relationship:

1. The mentor's task includes molding the character of the learner.

This is why the mentor's attitude plays a large part in the success of mentoring his pupil.

There's a proverbial truth that says "He who walks with wise men will be wise, but the companion of fools will be destroyed."

The mentoree will reflect his mentor. His character. His attitude.

The Bible says Peter and John were recognized as

having been with Jesus. Elisha was recognized as the one who (served) poured water on Elijah's hands.

Your associations today will determine who you are tomorrow; therefore, choose your mentor carefully. (We will talk more about this later.)

2. The mentor assists the learner in change.

The mentor/mentoree relationship will always produce change.

Sam Walton, founder of Wal-Mart, said one key to their success was that their people developed a low-resistance-to-change attitude. They remained flexible.

3. The mentoree is taught the concept of serving.

In the secular system there are defined levels of authority. In Matthew 20:25-28, Jesus teaches that principle. However, He goes on to the second part of that spiritual law: "Whoever wishes to become great among you shall be your servant." In other words, the way to the top begins with serving.

4. The mentor motivates his mentoree to greater achievement.

The mentor does this through the process of what is commonly called "evaluation and affirmation." This means I evaluate the learner's progress and affirm his advancement with encouragement.

**It's been wisely said that we should
affirm publicly and evaluate privately.**

---

5. The mentor leads his student to a higher plateau of learning.

He does this by instilling within the mentoree a discipline to increase knowledge.

The first way this is accomplished is through reading. The mentor encourages his pupil to read. He teaches the concept that a leader is a reader.

Mentors will broaden the mentoree's intellectual boundaries by taking him to museums or concerts or lectures. Increased knowledge produces increased confidence.

6. The mentor assists his student to develop self-disciplines in every area of his life.

The successful mentoree learns spiritual, emotional, intellectual, social, material, and physical self-discipline.

The pupil is taught self-denial. The word disciple carries with it the concept of discipline. Any champion, regardless of his chosen field, realizes that the will to win is important, but the will to prepare through self-imposed disciplines is imperative.

7. The mentor practices the principle of "seed time and harvest."

As I sow into your life, I reap a harvest of like fruit in my own life. The mentor sows time, wisdom, effort, love, mercy, care, etc., and stands to reap a harvest of the same.

For example, the mentor encourages his underling to develop and pursue his dream. At the same time, the mentor is sowing seeds of his own dream that will end up producing a harvest in his own life. Remember, the mentor's goal is not personal increase but the increase of the mentoree. There's a biblical principle that teaches that decrease precedes increase.

Let me explain. In order to harvest I must sow or decrease my seed. He who sows much, harvests (or increases) much, the Bible says. Conversely, he who sows little, increases little.

As a mentor, I "decrease" by my giving into the life of another. I, therefore, position myself for increase!

8. *The mentor cultivates perseverance in the life of his learner.*

The parent says, "Do your homework."

The sales manager/mentor encourages "one more call." The marketing mentor says: "I don't care how many times you've shown the plan, make three more appointments."

The pastor says, "Keep on praying."

Larry Byrd, former Boston Celtic super-champion, says it best: "Push yourself again and again. . . . Don't give an inch until the final buzzer sounds."

I have a friend who says, "Quitting is a permanent solution to a temporary problem."

You will note a truth being replayed throughout this book: The mentor doesn't just teach or lead, but he *grows* people. This process can cause discomfort, stress, and even pain for the mentoree.

The results, however, can be electrifying and so rewarding.

Remember the square bamboo? The mentor "squares" off his pupil by "clamping" on him the mold he will end up reflecting. The square bamboo is the most precious and valuable. It's turned into a beautiful surprise.

The mentor molds "beautiful surprises," too!

Chapter Three

Wants, Needs, and the Big Five

In the movie *Chariots of Fire*, the character Abraham, an aspiring young track star, had experienced many moments of frustration. Try as he might, he was unable to acquire that "little extra" he needed to move himself up to the winner's circle.

He was convinced he was a champion, and if he could just find the right coach he could experience the thrill of breaking the tape at the finish line. Abraham found the man. A world-renowned track coach.

As the Jewish youngster discussed his desires with this somewhat cynical and grizzled running master, the coach looked at him and said, "I can't get out of you what God has not put in you."

That's why mentors are God's gift to young aspirants. Mentors don't concentrate on what is *not* in their mentorees, but seek to cultivate what *is* in them so the strengths are allowed to flourish and produce fruit.

What are people looking for in a mentor-mentoree relationship?

Most of us, like Abraham, want three basic things from the mentoring process:

Success

Like most of us, Abraham was looking for success. He wanted a coach/mentor who would help him achieve that success.

The coach/mentor creates a winning atmosphere. He encourages his mentoree to shine through his strengths.

Improvement

Abraham recognized he needed two or three more steps in a shorter distance if he was to be the champion he desired to be. He wanted a mentor who could be the force behind his life to help him get away from the starting blocks a half-step quicker, a fraction of a second faster.

People submit to mentors because they want their shortcomings met.

Practical help

Almost everyone, including Abraham, wants a relationship with a mentor who will provide practical skills to assist them in constructing their lives.

Just as a worker needs skills and a description of what is expected of him on his job, the mentoree is also looking for specific tools designed to build his life.

What People Need

One way the mentor accomplishes this is by recognizing the five needs that people have in their lives.

Let's look at these five needs:

People need consistency. The effective mentor is not one way one day and the other the next. He is always consistent in behavior, attitudes, and in the way he conducts his life.

Children, especially, need consistent discipline from their parents. New Christians need to see more mature saints consistently living out their beliefs. Employees need to be trained by more experienced workers who don't waver in their principles.

People need approachability. Whether we are parents, in company management, or some other leadership position, those under our authority need to see us as believable, open, and transparent. We communicate genuine care and concern when we're approachable by those who are looking to us for guidance.

People need confidence in their leadership management. That confidence is instilled when people trust the character of those whom they follow.

In addition, we need to show confidence in our

followers in order for them to become more confident of their abilities.

People don't buy into *your* dream or *your* plans. They buy into *you*, and you buy into *their* dreams.

People must have confidence in who you are as a person.

People need direction. Foresight sets leaders apart from their followers. People need others who will point them in the right direction.

Leaders see things differently than their followers. They see through the eye of opportunity. Leaders are trailblazers plotting the course for those coming behind.

People need leadership that is energetic and enthusiastic. The depth of your conviction — not the height of your logic — convinces people of your dedication to them and your common cause.

You can only motivate others if you exhibit sincere enthusiasm in the mentoring process. Don't become critical if your mentoree isn't progressing as quickly as you had hoped. Instead, look for ways to instill new energy into the training process.

The Big Five

The practice of mentoring deals with our most

valuable asset — people. Not projects or profit and loss statements, but people.

Frequently, leadership becomes so involved in the affairs and the administration of the organization, we forget that our eventual responsibility rests in mentoring people.

Leadership in every walk of life would be wise to give heed to the philosophy of General Norman Schwarzkopf as presented in his autobiography, *It Doesn't Take A Hero.*[1]

When General Norm was promoted to division commander early in his career, he was searching for an effective leadership plan that would equip him for his new role.

After much deliberation he came up with what he describes as the "Big Five" principles of leadership that he felt he needed to follow as a division commander.

Here are Schwarzkopf's "Big Five:"

- Make sure my division is combat ready.
- Take care of the soldiers.
- Take care of the soldiers' families.
- Encourage and develop loyalty from one soldier to the other.
- Mentor my subordinates just as I have been mentored.

Stormin' Norman had learned that these principles were the motivation that caused soldiers to fight. Cohesiveness and camaraderie, the general realized, were absolutely necessary among the troops. The focus of mentoring was to develop a high standard of ethics among his people.

These five sure-fire helps were seen to be effective in the general's leadership during the military activity in the Gulf War.

These same Desert Storm leadership principles can be applied to our relationships with people in our workplace, our home, and our church as well.

We too, must focus on people — preparing them, equipping them, caring for them and their families, encouraging a cohesiveness among them, and mentoring them.

In an interview with *INC. Magazine*, the general expanded his views on the "Big Five." Let's look at them:

1. Have clearly defined goals and be able to articulate them to others so they're able to comprehend them.

2. Establish for yourself a clear agenda. Every morning, the general writes down the five most important things he needs to accomplish that day.

3. Let your people know where they stand. Stay in touch and communicate with them so they don't question where they stand with you or your organization.

4. Don't procrastinate. Leaders fix what's broken *when* it's broken. Problems not dealt with will simply multiply.

5. No repainting the flagpole. Make sure

the work being done by the people in your organization is productive and vital.

6. Set high standards. People's performance rarely exceeds the standard you expect of them.

7. Lay your concepts and plans out to your people, but let them execute them.

8. Never lie. NEVER. EVER.

9. When in charge, take command. This includes being decisive, not double minded. Provide security for your followers by using your authority wisely.

10. Do what's right. The truth is we always know the right thing to do. The hard part is in the doing.

As a leader, General Swartzkoff realized he must also function as a mentor. These principles of leadership are a part of his curriculum for his mentorees. We would do well to emulate his example.

Using Goose Sense

In the fall when you see geese in a "V" formation, heading back south for the winter, you might be interested to know why they fly that way. Scientists have learned that as each bird flaps its wings, it creates an uplift for the bird immediately following.

By flying in a "V" formation, the whole flock adds at least 71 percent more flying range than if each bird were on its own.

What does this teach us about the importance of mentoring? Several principles can be formulated from the example of our geese friends. When we seek a mentoring relationship with someone whom we respect and admire, we add more "range" to our life.

God has created man with a natural need for dependence. This is not a sign of weakness, but a sign of wisdom. Mentoring fulfills that need.

We also acquire a dependable support system. When a goose gets sick or is wounded and falls out of formation, two geese fall out with the goose and follow it down to provide help and protection. They stay with it until it is either able to fly or is dead.

The mentor provides the support when the mentoree can't make it on his own. When he falls out wounded, tired, beaten up, or beat down, his mentor will not forsake him. He'll stand by him through thick and thin.

Learning where to turn for help is another key. Whenever a goose falls out of formation, it suddenly feels drag and air resistance from trying to go it alone. It quickly gets back into formation to take advantage of the lifting power of the bird immediately in front.

The mentoree is dependent on the mentor. The mentor keeps the protégé from handling all the resistance by himself by lifting him and building him up. The student quickly learns that getting back into the mentors formation will keep him "aloft."

And never underestimate positive reinforcement. The geese honk from behind to encourage those up front to keep their speed. The mentor keeps honking at the mentoree to keep up. Honk! Honk!

He or she also teaches responsibility. When the lead goose gets tired, it rotates back in the wing and another flies point. Mentors and mentorees learn quickly that we should learn to take turns on hard jobs.

Now that you understand the importance of mentoring, you can determine where you fit into the picture — either as one who needs a mentor in certain areas of your life or one who is able to mentor another person.

Whatever your needs or abilities, your potential can be more fully realized through the mentoring process, whether it happens in your home, in the church, or in the marketplace — or all three!

Part 2

Coaching Your Own Champions

Chapter Four

Dad and Mom as Mentors

"If your children were small again, what would you do?"

These words burst from the heart of a father sitting across from me who felt he had failed.

I thought of my own father. What did he do that made him so special?

My dad was my hero. He was a simple man, but a man of great character.

My dad's father ran off with a circus that came through town when my dad was just three years old. My father's older brothers and sisters left home early in their lives, leaving just my dad and his mother to make it on their own.

At the age of five, my pop started to work clean-

ing spittoons in a local pool hall. Then, at the end of
third grade, he had to quit school to work full-time to
support his mother.

Later he joined the military. At the end of World
War I, he returned to his hometown, went to work for
the railroad, met my mom, and married her.

A few years later, a car accident severely deformed
his left arm, making it almost useless. He was unable
to do his regular job. Because of his work record and
his diligence, however, the railroad transferred him to
a foreman's position at a company-owned stock yard.

My father worked that job for 40-plus years from
eight o'clock at night until seven in the morning, seven
nights a week. His only time off was a two-week vaca-
tion every year.

Yet, with this kind of work schedule I never once
heard him complain. I never heard him feel sorry for
himself.

When he came home in the morning he would
wake me up, and I would sit on his lap to have a cup of
hot cocoa. We rarely spoke a word to one another. I
just sat on his lap. He put his arm around me and was
just there.

I cherished those few moments with my dad so
much that we continued the tradition until I got so big
I thought we would have to trade places!

In spite of his incredible work schedule, his family still received his foremost attention. He taught me
hunting, took me fishing, and often would take me with
him to work.

Dad realized that character is more often caught
than taught. What he wanted most for me was that I

reflect the character traits he admired in others and had developed in his life.

My father's "mentoring" effect in my life inspired me to do a Father's Day sermon a number of years ago called "What I Would Do Differently If I Were Doing It Again."

I pondered my own parenting shortcomings and came up with a few suggestions that will assist today's mentor-dads.

If I Could Parent My Children All Over Again

I would love the mother of my children more.

That is, I would be more free to let my children see that I love her. I would seek to be faithful in doing little loving things for her like opening the car door, placing her chair at the table, giving her little gifts on special occasions, and writing her love letters when I'm away from home.

I would take her hand as we stroll in the park and would praise her in the presence of my children. A child who knows that his parents love each other has a security and stability about life gained in no other way.

"Husbands, love your wives, just as Christ also loved the church and gave Himself up for her" (Eph. 5:25).

I would be a better listener.

Most fathers find it hard to listen. We are busy with the burdens of work, and at the end of the day we are tired.

I would listen when my child shares his little hurts and complaints and what he is excited about. And I would try to refrain from words of impatience at the interruption. Such times can be the best times to show love and kindness.

One evening a small boy tried to show his father a scratch on his finger. Finally, after the boy's repeated attempts to gain his father's attention, the father stopped reading his newspaper and said impatiently. "Well, I can't do anything about it, can I?"

"Yes, Daddy," his small son said, "you could have said 'Oh.' "

I would try to understand what my child says because the father who listens to his child when he is small will find that he will have a child who cares what his father says later in life.

In listening, I would pay more careful attention to my child's questions. It is estimated that the average child asks 500,000 questions by the age of 15. What an opportunity for every parent to teach about the meaning of life and your dependence on God!

I would seek more opportunities to give my child a feeling of belonging.

When a child feels he belongs in his family and is of real worth there, it is easy for him to also feel accepted, loved, and of worth to others and in God's sight. A child feels he belongs when he is involved in the responsibility and work of the family.

Celebration of birthdays creates a sense of belonging, especially when the person rather than the gift, is the center of things. That same sense is built into the child when he hears prayers prayed on his behalf. No part of child guidance is more important than making him feel he has a place in the affections of the family.

"Behold, children are a heritage from the Lord, The fruit of the womb is His reward" (Ps. 127:3).

I would express words of appreciation and praise more.

Many children seldom hear words of commendation and encouragement when they do a job well or exhibit good behavior.

Will Sessions, discussing the topic "If I Had a Teenager" says, "I would bestow praise. If the youngster blew a horn, I would try to find at lease one note that sounded good to my ear, and I would say a sincere good word about it. If the school theme was to my liking, I would say so, hoping that it would get a good grade when it was turned in. . . . I would be vocal."

Probably no other thing encourages a child to love life, to seek accomplishment, and to gain confidence more than proper, sincere praise; not flattery, but honest compliments when he does well.

"See that you do not look down on one of these little ones" (Matt. 18:10).

I would spend more time together.

A group of 300 seventh and eighth grade boys kept accurate records of how much time their fathers actually spent with them over a two-week period. Most saw their father only at the dinner table. A number never saw their father for days at a time. The average time a father and son were alone for an entire week was 7 1/2 minutes!

Arthur Gordon tells an interesting experience from his youth.

When I was around 13 and my brother

was 10, Father promised to take us to the circus. But at lunch there was a phone call; some urgent business required his attention downtown. My brother and I braced ourselves for the disappointment. Then we heard him say, "No, I won't be down. It will have to wait."

When he came back to the table, Mother smiled. "The circus keeps coming back, you know."

"I know," said Father, "but childhood doesn't."

"Making the most of every opportunity, because the days are evil" (Eph. 5:16).

If I were to start my family again, I would laugh more. That's right!

I remember when I laughed with my children at the humorous plays they put on for the family, at the funny stories shared from school, at the times I fell for their tricks and catch questions. I recall the squeals of delight when I laughed with them and shared in their stunts on the lawn or living room floor.

I know when I laughed with my children, our love was enlarged and the door was open for doing many other things together.

"A cheerful heart is good medicine, but a crushed spirit dries up the bones" (Prov. 17:22).

Tell Me Your Hopes and Dreams

Somehow we manage enough muscle to handle the big things of life but forget that life is largely made up of little things. A father's faithfulness in the small things determines the happiness of his children. It also strongly influences their character development.

"And you, fathers, do not provoke your children to wrath, but bring them up in the training and admonition of the Lord" (Eph. 6:4).

Not too long ago, my son-in-law sat down with my granddaughter, Kelly, and told her to pretend that he was God and he wanted her to talk with him about her hopes and dreams.

Her beautiful 15-year-old (almost 16) eyes got as big as saucers.

"Now," said my son-in-law, holding up his wrist and grinning at her, then squinting at his watch, "Tell me your hopes and dreams — in 60 seconds."

"Well," she mused. And then, she rattled off the aspirations she had for her life: her education goals, her career ambitions, her future family hopes.

Do you know what was really going on between this loving father and his beloved daughter?

Mentoring.

He was showing her just how much our Almighty Father cares about our wants and needs.

But my son-in-law was doing something else, too. He was listening and showing an interest in Kelly's relationship to God and to her relationship with him.

She was a little uncomfortable with the whole idea at first — as most teenage girls would be. But she quickly caught on to the purpose of why her dad was doing what he did.

Wouldn't it be wonderful if all relationships could be as simple and trusting as that between a father and his teenage daughter? A dad is, in many ways, the closest thing to God that a child knows.

He is her protector.

He is her provider.

He is her teacher.

And he loves her deeply.

What he says is important to her.

She likes pleasing him.

He is, on multiple levels, her *mentor*.

The Greater Gift

Comedian David Brenner grew up poor in Philadelphia. He never expected a graduation gift when he finished high school, yet he received a gift that impacted his life in a special way.

Brenner points out that many of his friends received cars, tuition for college, or new clothes. He was just pleased his family could be there to see him receive his diploma.

After the graduation, David's dad said to him, "I have your graduation gift," and extended his closed hand toward his son. "Here it is," he said.

When David put out his hand, palm up, Dad Brenner let the graduation gift drip into his son's hand. What was it? A nickel!

With that, David's father advised, "Buy a newspaper with the nickel. Read every word from front to back, turn to the classified section, and find yourself a job. The world is all yours now."

It wasn't until years later that David Brenner realized the significance of that graduation gift.

When he was in the military, he began meditating about his life, and a thought suddenly dawned on him:

His friends had received their cars, clothes, and college tuition, but he had received the greater gift. His dad had given him the whole world.

Brenner said, "The day I made that discovery I became a man."[1]

Inspiring Champions

At the 1960 Olympic Games in Rome, Italy, Wilma Rudolph dreamed of a gold medal.

One of 22 children, Wilma had been stricken with polio at a very young age. Fitted with braces, she was unable to run and play like the other kids. Wilma was handicapped.

Wilma, however, had a "mentor-mom" who was determined to encourage her daughter to strive for championship status.

Wilma herself says: "My mother taught me very early to believe I could achieve any accomplishment I wanted to. The first was to walk without braces."

At the age of 10, Wilma walked out of her braces into a whole new life. With this newfound freedom, she spent all her time running and playing. Soon she began to excel in basketball and track.

Her athletic ability won her a berth on the 1960 U.S. Olympic Track Team. This 20-year-old girl, who had been able to walk without braces for only 10 years, became the first woman to win three gold medals in Olympic track and field.

Wilma said of her mentoring mom: "She was the one who made me work."

When asked why she didn't run as a pro, she put it this way: "My interests now are my family . . . and the kids I'm working with. Now I'm trying to develop other champions."[2]

Are you a mentoring-mom? There's a champion in your home ready to be motivated, inspired, and encouraged to believe he or she can achieve. Inspire your son or daughter to go for the gold.

Lillian Carter, mother of former President Jimmy Carter is quoted as saying: "If I had only one wish for my children, it would be that each of them would reach for goals that have meaning for them as individuals."

You don't have to be a supermom or superdad to be a mentoring parent.

"I'm not an American Hero, I'm a person who loves children." Those words, spoken by "Mother" Clara McBride Hale when she was named an American Hero by President Reagan in 1985, sum up the job of being a parent — love your children and encourage them to do their best. The rest is up to them.

Chapter Five

Tender/Tough Mentoring

Since 1968, Americans have looked to the Commerce Departments' Index of Leading Economic Indicators to spot economic trends.

Now former U.S. Education Secretary William Bennett has complied a list of "social indicators." He says they point to a strong decline in American cultural values.

One particular Bennett list, which appeared in the March 29, 1993, issue of *Time Magazine*, points to the following:

• Teen suicide has increased from 3.6 (per 100,000 teens) in 1960 to 11.3 (per 100,000 teens) in 1990.

• Average TV viewing per household has increased 2 hours per day in the last 30 years.
• Violent crimes have increased nearly 5 times since 1960.
• In 1960, 5.3 percent of births in this nation were to unwed mothers. In 1990 it was 28 percent.
• Average SAT scores have dropped from 975 to 899 since 1960.

The concept of family mentoring is one answer to turning the family crisis situation around. If parents can learn to apply mentoring techniques in their home, we could soon see a reversal in the deteriorating American household.

Seven Common Mistakes Parents Make

Let me share some common mistakes that parents frequently make with teens. This list is not all-inclusive but simply a means to encourage you to evaluate your parenting style.

Mistake 1: Threatening as a by-product of anger.

Idle threats mean little and cause a credibility gap between you and your child.

Mistake 2: Excessive expectations.

The effects of setting achievement goals too high for your children have a tendency to produce discouragement on their part.

Mistake 3: Nagging.

Constant disapproval of trivial issues will drive a

wedge between you and your teenager.

Mistake 4: Overlooking irresponsible behavior.

Not dealing with lost books, forgotten school assignments, missed curfews, and other irresponsible habits now will later create a tardy, unorganized adult who finds it difficult to achieve success.

Mistake 5: Avoiding discussion of uncomfortable issues.

If you as a parent don't confront issues like sex, drugs, dating, etc., — first — you can bet someone else will beat you to the punch.

Mistake 6: Humiliating your teen in front of others.

Avoid disciplining your child in front of anyone. Don't use discipline as a power-play to show others you are in control.

Mistake 7: Eroding their self-value.

Place the emphasis on the action and not on the person. Instead of saying, "You're stupid," say, "That was an irresponsible thing to do."

We pay a price when we deprive children of the exposure to values, principles, and education they need to make them good citizens. The family plays a critical role in our society and in the training of the generation to come.

Tender/Tough Mentoring Rules

In every mentoring relationship there is a time of confrontation, when a "tough" approach is necessary to deal with certain issues. Parent mentors realize that the tough times need to be tenderized in order for positive results to be obtained.

Parents would be wise to learn these tender/tough mentoring rules. These principles could help to eliminate some of the mistakes in dealing with your teens. Let's look at them:

Rule 1: Get to the point quickly.

Mentoring confrontations are always direct and specific. Don't beat around the bush in generalities and don't lecture for hours on end.

Rule 2: Demonstrate unconditional love.

Love cannot be based on your child's performance. Before and after confrontation re-affirm your relationship and love.

Rule 3: Always consider relationships ahead of issues.

What your child is wearing, or his earring on his ear, may be an issue, but don't allow it to separate or divide your relationship.

Rule 4: Praise in public; correct in private.

Mentoring parents do not embarrass or humiliate their children in front of others.

Rule 5: Encourage your child's strong points.

Mentors help unlock the achievement of others by building on their strengths through positive edification.

Don't be constantly focused on your child's negative traits.

Rule 6: Try to see the issue from the child's point of view.

Mentors deal with their mentorees from a position of empathy not power. Parental authority is not justification for abusive power. Take some time and listen to your children from their viewpoint.

Rule 7. Mentors discipline and don't punish.

Discipline encourages growth; punishment produces a slave mentality. Discipline encourages positive learning; punishment stimulates rebellion.

When we discipline our children we are teaching or instructing them. Discipline is a learning experience. Punishment, on the other hand, is frequently meted out to satisfy our own frustration or demands.

We all want to raise perfect kids. Too often we base our skills at raising children on how well or how badly our children behave.

"The problems are variations on two themes," according to Nancy Samalier, founder of Parent Guidance Workshops in New York City, "seeing our children as reflections of ourselves . . . and having unrealistic expectations."

Let's not heap "coals of condemnation" on our heads for our parenting shortcomings or wring our hands because our kids are less than perfect. Let's concentrate instead on becoming "mentoring parents."

Let me make some simple suggestions for the mentoring parent that can be used to help you in developing your little champions.

• *Teach them to accept self-responsibility.*

Discourage blame placing. Cause your kids to recognize they can't go through life always blaming others for their mistakes.

• *Encourage staying-power.*

Teach follow-through. Frequently, our kids will decide they want to take dance lessons, drum lessons, swimming lessons, or whatever. But, after a while, when they're bored, they want to quit and do something else. Don't allow them to quit in mid-stream. Set a time period and tell them they must stay until they finish.

• *Instruct them in the importance of goal-setting.*

Make the goals realistic, taking into account the age and maturity of their youth. Maybe a goal for your youngster could involve household chores, schoolwork, athletics, Bible reading, whatever. The potential is limitless.

Goals come in short-term objectives (one week, one month, three months); mid-term time periods (six months, one year) or long-term (five years, ten years).

• *Teach the importance of values and the self-disciplines of life necessary to develop them.*

Spiritual, emotional, intellectual, physical, social, and material disciplines are a part of the curriculum of would-be champions.

Sandra Day O'Connor, the first woman to sit on the Supreme Court, shares this thought: "We pay a price when we deprive children of the exposure to values, principles, and education they need to make them good citizens. The family plays a critical role in our society and in the training of the generation to come."

• *Encourage your youngsters to take part in life.*

They'll never know whether they can or can't until they try. Let your aspiring champ learn that the essential goal in life is not conquering, but doing our very best. The Olympic Creed, in part, puts it this way:

The important thing in the Olympic games is not winning, but taking part.

Teach them that life can be a wonderful adventure. Whether it's in church, on the ball team, in the classroom, at home, wherever — adventure is worthwhile in itself.

How Does Your Family Compare?

A study several years ago by two sociologists at Harvard developed a test to identify crucial factors in the delinquent behavior of juveniles.

As a result of the study, four factors were discovered that would help greatly in reducing or preventing delinquency.

1. The fathers' discipline must be firm, fair, and consistent.

2. Mothers' supervision must be to spend

time with the children, but she also must know where they are and what they're doing at all times.

3. The children should see affection demonstrated between Mom and Dad, and experience affection aimed at them.

4. The family's cohesiveness should be experienced by the kids. The family spending time together is vital.

Implementation of these four simple factors are being challenged on every front in today's culture. Even our own family lifestyles are frequently a threat to accomplishing the above suggestions.

In examining the condition of the American family today we find some interesting trends. For example, when Family Research Council surveyed a group of randomly-selected adults, they found 72 percent who said changes in family lifestyle over the past three decades "have been generally for the worse."

Sixty percent of those polled said "children are generally worse off today than when they (the parents) were children."

More than half (52 percent) of all men believe children are "worse off" today than when they were growing up. This is opposed to 68 percent of women who believe that way.

Please note: Most analysts believe the vast difference in opinions (16 percent) between male and females reflect the fact men are less likely to be involved than women in the day-to-day lives of children. In addition, men are more likely to view questions regarding "well-being" from an economic perspective.

Through the Eyes of a Child

What else is America saying about family issues? Let's look further into the matter by examining another set of statistics made available through Family Research Council.[1]

Five issues were presented to a group of adults. The issues were:

- Divorce
- Illegitimacy
- Day Care
- Pornography
- Abortion

These adults first were asked to view these issues through the eyes of children and respond accordingly. Here are the results:

- 93 percent believe "children suffer when parents divorce."
- 83 percent believe "it's better for a child to be born into a two-parent situation than to a single mom."
- 87 percent think the child is better off under the care of mother than day care.
- 84 percent believe pornography is harmful to kids.
- 64 percent believe unborn children should have a right to life.

Note, however, when these same people were asked to express the views on the same issues through the eyes of an adult, the results were quite different.

- 51 percent say couples should seek divorce if the marriage is not working.
- 56 percent believe women should be able to have children out of wedlock without being judged.
- 27 percent believe moms should resume to the work force and place the children in day care.
- 14 percent say there should be no restrictions on sexually explicit materials and entertainment.
- 67 percent say women should have the right to choose abortion.

After examining these responses, one should conclude that many issues dividing our nation could be resolved if people would agree the needs of children should supersede the wants of adults.

That brings us back again to mentoring in the home. Mentoring provides the platform in the home that encourages the teaching of ethics and values to our children. It must begin at home.

Chapter Six

The Family Mentoring Session

Let's take a look at the approach to family mentoring that's working in one modern household.

The Jerrolds have three children ages seven, nine, and eleven. They have arranged a family mentoring session for one night a week (usually Monday night).

As threatening as the term "Family Mentoring Session" may be, it's really just a time for the family to be together to do some specific activities uninterrupted and in an environment of fun.

The Jerrolds give these suggestions as to how to make the "sessions" fun and profitable.

• Set a time limit on how long the meeting can last — 30 minutes maximum.

• All family members should consider the get-together a priority on their schedule.

• Establish a regular day and time for the session so everyone can plan their time schedules accordingly.

• Use the sessions to discuss the family calendar of activities for the week, individual plans, etc.

• Mention a certain character value, discuss it, and put it into practice for the week. For example, if the character trait of "unselfishness" is the topic, someone explains it, gives appropriate examples, then a general discussion follows. The specific "value" is written on a 3 x 5 card and given to each family member, who then agrees to practice the trait at home, at work, and with a friend all week. At the following week's session, the family discusses the results of the practice.

• Make each child feel special and important. Encourage everyone to actively participate. The kids should know that their input is respected.

• Make fun the watch word.

The Jerrolds don't use the mentoring time to deal with controversial or potentially negative situations. The environment and atmosphere is aimed at an enjoyable learning experience.

The result? The parents agree that since implementing this mentoring method, relationships in the home are more meaningful; the kids feel more a part of the whole family; and the youngsters are more sensitive to the character found in other people.

Frequently the Jerrolds' kids are overheard commenting about the untruthfulness they observed in someone else, or the lack of courtesy one of their friends displayed.

Lois Jerrold puts it this way: "We've established 12 positive character traits we want to see our family demonstrate. By having our mentoring meetings each week, we're able to teach, apply, and reinforce these values at least four different times a year."

The Jerrolds' family mentoring method is working in their home to produce the quality lifestyle that God intends for the family unit.

Such a concept requires great commitment and purpose on the part of each family member. The time, the schedules, and the agenda all demand that the 30 minutes of family mentoring must be a priority.

If I Had a Dad

"I don't have a dad," says Carrie, age seven. "Well, I guess I do have a dad, I just don't know his name."

Carrie, who lives with her mother and 12-year-old brother in Kansas, *does* know what fathers do, though.

"They kiss you and hug you when you need them. They show you love and care. They talk to you. I wish I had somebody to talk to me."

What would Carrie do if she did have a dad at home?

Carrie answers: "I'd sit on his lap and smell his aftershave. We'd look at TV together, play games, and take a walk with each other."

The number of single-parent households has increased by 20 percent in the last 20 years, from four million to somewhere around eight million today, according to the Census Bureau.

The number of working moms rose from 10.2 million to 16.8 million in the same 20 years. That is an increase of 65 percent, the Bureau of Labor Statistics notes.

This increase in single-parent homes has fostered other statistics, producing a grim picture of our society. One, in particular, makes the point: The FBI reports an estimated 70 percent of juvenile offenders come from single-parent families.

Researchers tracking the lives of children of divorced parents discovered these characteristics in some, if not all, of the kids:

- Moderate to severe depression for as long as 5 years after the split.
- After 10 years, a significant number appeared to be troubled, drifting, and underachieving.
- After 15 years, many were struggling to create strong love relationships of their own.
- Children of divorce are twice as likely to drop out of school.
- Daughters of divorced parents frequently have a difficult time exercising good

judgment in choosing marriage partners.
• For boys of divorced parents, the critical issue is role modeling.

It's a Character Problem

Whether you're a single dad or single mom, the job of being effective in raising your children to be productive citizens is a mammoth challenge. Learning how to mentor your children, however, could make all the difference in the direction their lives take — in spite of what the statistics say.

A parent, however, is not automatically a mentor just because of their position. Family mentoring is a deliberate act on the part of both parent and child.

Parents frequently are tied to certain learned and pre-supposed or inherited concepts of what dads and moms are supposed to be and do. Unfortunately, our role models have not always been correct.

Many single parents think the mentor/child relationship belongs to someone else — like the school teacher, the coach, the Sunday school superintendent.

The problem in today's society is not so much violence, sex, and abuse — it's a character problem. Understanding the parental/mentor role will equip and motivate single parents to emphasize the need to nurture positive character development in their children.

I've talked to single parents who have said that the concept of mentoring helped relieve some of the burden of parenting because they too frequently viewed their role as a disciplinarian. Setting aside a specific mentoring time allowed them to have a more objective relationship with their child.

Developing a Mentoring/Child Program

"Pastor, mentoring is wonderful even if it does have to be forced for awhile."

These words came from a 28-year-old single mom whose life is busy with her job, her two children, and her ministry in a local church.

Financially, she has no choice but to work outside the home. Her children are both school-aged and are well-adapted, considering the absence of a father in the home.

Michelle (not her real name), after learning about the principles of mentoring, decided to apply the techniques and philosophy in helping her fulfill her responsibilities to her children.

The results, she says, have been gratifying.

Michelle began by listing the goals that she wanted the mentoring/child program to attain.

She talked to her children and observed their true behavior at home. She also counseled with her children's babysitter to get her observations regarding the kids. From that "research" her goals were established for each of her children.

Next, she determined the system that would be most effective for her family. Michelle decided to set apart a Saturday morning every two weeks to spend time with each of the children individually. Furthermore, after each six sessions there would be a three-week break for her and the children.

She also realized that adjustments might be necessary along the way.

Heart-to-Heart

The sessions were designated as heart-to-heart time. Mom allowed the kids to share their heart with her openly without fear or intimidation. Michelle pointed out it took much prodding and several sessions before the youngsters began to open up.

The number one emphasis of these heart-to-heart sessions was to re-affirm their relationship with one another, promoting security between mom and child. She also took time to reassure the kids that they were totally accepted and loved with no strings attached.

Homemaking skills were also taught to the children, and etiquette and social graces were encouraged. Self-esteem was emphasized, and even sports knowledge and athletic participation were a part of heart-to-heart.

Michelle has this to say about her mentoring experiment: "Heart-to-heart has been a trying time for all of us, but I'm so glad we're committed to seeing it through. We've cried a lot, but laughed a whole lot more."

The mentoring/parental application of child growth and development requires a new way of thinking about your relationships. The process does require ingenuity, creativity, and imagination on the part of everyone involved.

No matter how you approach the mentoring process in your home, parents can create a powerful bonding between themselves and their children if they're willing to pay the price.

Chapter Seven

If Not You —
You —
Who?

At the age of 15, while working at an early morning before-school janitor's job at Young's Pharmacy in Emporia, Kansas, I learned about character.

Mr. Young didn't trust anybody — especially teenage janitor/stock boys. He was really a tormentor. I either didn't work fast enough, thoroughly enough, or long enough.

One early morning, before the store had opened, I was busily sweeping behind the counter where the cash register sat. All of a sudden I saw it!

A beautiful, crisp $10 bill. Now remember, in

1950, $10 was really . . . well, $10!

There it was, just waiting for me to pick it up. What I could do with $10! Visions of sugar plums danced through my head!

The boss was in the basement. No one else in the store. Should I or shouldn't I?

All of a sudden it dawned on me. My trustworthiness was being revealed. My action at that precise moment would shed light on who I was and what I was!

My parents had done much to develop positive character traits in my life. One of which was honesty. I couldn't keep that $10 bill. No way.

I picked it up, ran to the basement, and presented it proudly to good ole Mr. Young. I just knew I was in for a handsome reward because of my truthfulness.

It didn't quite work out that way.

He didn't even say thanks. He just turned away, grumbling over the fact that somebody apparently had been careless when closing out the register.

I really did have my reward though. The crisis had revealed that I possessed an inner-strength that I would not compromise.

My parents had prepared me for that moment in my life. They had instilled within me as a child the character traits that would be tested over and over as I went through life.

**Crisis is not the developer of character,
but the greatest revealer of character.**

The Missing Ingredient

In a recent survey done by the Josephson Institute of Ethics, one-third of high school students admitted they had stolen something from a store, 61 percent had cheated on an exam, 35 percent had made serious ethnic slurs, and 20 percent had driven while drunk — all within the past year.

We've included this section on character because we believe, in the final analysis, the primary effect of a mentoring relationship is character development.

A teacher imparts knowledge and instruction. A leader inspires and directs. But a mentor imparts all of these things and much more. He imparts his life. The mentor molds the character of the learner. This is never more apparent than in the family relationships.

Thomas Carlyle said:

Be what you would have your pupil to be.

What do we mean when we talk character? It's defined in many ways. Here are a few:

- A distinctive mark, trait, or quality. A pattern of behavior.
- A collection of personal beliefs and how we act on them.
- Character is the sum total of our every day choices.[2]

Let me share a portion of an editorial from the

Washington Post written by Judy Mann that illustrates the crisis facing American families today: (The particular incident referred to occurred outside Washington, DC.)

> Michael Josephson, president of the Joseph and Edna Josephson Institute of Ethics, had the same reaction a lot of us had to the story about the parents who rented buses to transport teenagers to a party at a North Potomac home last Friday night.
> He was outraged.
> The story on the front page of Wednesday's *Washington Post* was yet another example of parents sending mixed messages to young people about drinking by underage kids and enabling illegal behavior ostensibly so the kids wouldn't drink and drive.
> Those of us with teenagers know that a house without parents can become a party house if the resident teenager is left behind. In this case, the party was also facilitated by another set of parents who went away, leaving their 16- and 17-year-old sons alone. The unchaperoned beer blast started about midnight, right after a homecoming dance. Police broke it up after neighbors complained, and the episode is now on the growing list of instances in which teenagers have gotten out of hand.

Michael Josephson (whom the editorial refers to)

is founder of a Character Counts Coalition, hoping to reach 20 million young people with a clear-cut message of ethics and character.

Mr. Josephson and other leaders in business, education, and the church are fast coming to the conclusion there is an ethics and character crisis facing our nation today.

In the final analysis the issue is clear. The development of an ethical character is of prime importance in this nation. It isn't just a "kid" issue or a parent issue, it's an "everybody" issue. That's why the concept of biblical mentoring is such an encouraging force today.

A Few Good Character Traits

Let me make a few simple suggestions to parents as to the specific character traits that should be given attention to in our lives and the lives of others.

1. Honesty
Good old-fashioned honesty means:
- Integrity
- Loyalty
- Keeping your word
- Trustworthiness

Someone once wisely said it this way: Promises kept — deadlines met — commitments honored. Not just for the sake of old-fashioned morality, but because we become what we do (or fail to do), and character is simply the sum of our performances.

2. Responsibility
We understand responsibility to mean:
- Self-discipline

- To be answerable and accountable
- Citizenship
- Family

I believe that excuse-making for our behavior is simply natural man's attempt at justifying inaction and eluding self-responsibility.

3. Caring, compassion, and mercy

This simply means: Doing unto others as you would have them do unto you.

4. Respect of life and property

"The less we emphasize the Christian religion, the further we fall into the abyss of poor character and chaos" (Mississippi Governor Kirk Fordyce).

5. Work ethic

The effort to strive for:
- Excellence
- Dependability
- Enthusiasm

"If we're to restore the work ethic, the first step is to teach . . . the difference between right and wrong, good and evil and there is a virtue and value and dignity in work" (*Why America Doesn't Work,* Chuck Colson and Jack Eckerd).[3]

6. Perseverance

Defined as:
- Tenacity
- Courage
- Steadfastness
- Refusal to give up

Thomas Jefferson put it this way: "In matter of style, swim the current; in matter of principle, stand like a rock."

7. Faith
Living a life of:
- Confidence
- Assurance
- Positiveness

Faith, hope, and love are the three "theological" virtues in the Christian character.

I suppose the list could go on and on. All of us would have our own "list" of virtues, our own concept of character values that we feel deeply about. This was not intended to be an all-inclusive inventory, but a stimulating "jolt" into the need to begin to consider values and ethics in our homes, schools, and workplace.

Consider this well-known quote on character:

Whatever a man loves most, governs him. If he loves pleasure most, his character is sensual. If he loves money most, his character is worldly. If he loves knowledge most, his character is philosophical. But if he loves God most, his character is divine *(Author unknown)*.

God our Father is more concerned with our character than our comfort. Shouldn't His example be ours? Shouldn't our concern for our family be more character building than comfort providing?

Mentoring relationships in the home should be

geared to developing positive character patterns in our children. Dad and/or Mom need to set aside a mentoring time when character training is emphasized.

If you don't, who will?

Part 3

*Kingdom
Mentoring*

Chapter Eight

The Ninth Wave

An ancient belief of the sea proposes that, inevitably, one wave comes along that is greater than any that has preceded it. It's called the "ninth wave."

To catch the ninth wave at the critical moment requires a special skill and sensitivity and timing.

Today, in the kingdom of God, we see such a powerful wave beginning to be revealed. The Church's own ninth wave brings with it significant change. Let's catch it and ride it all the way to the top.

As I travel today, I'm hearing with greater degree than ever before: "Things are changing." *Change,* however, is a word that frightens many in Christendom.

In your church, the change may involve the emphasis of your outreach. In another, the change may be in mode of worship. Whatever the change, it's designed for each individual ministry.

I'm not talking about a change in theology as much as a change in methodology. The same wonderful message of faith and hope in the gospel has not changed, but it is being presented today, as Jesus said, "in fresh wineskins."

More Time with Fewer People

The concept "more time with fewer people to create a lasting impact" originated with Jesus. He fed 5,000-plus people but spent time imparting himself to only 12 men.

That describes Kingdom mentoring — an impartation of one's life to another. Perhaps the most effective way this can be accomplished is one on one.

Jesus called "ordinary" people into the work of the ministry. The first Twelve were everyday men with jobs and families.

But Jesus had a plan.

He said, "Follow Me and I will make you fishers of men."

Jesus planned to make these ordinary people into extraordinary champions. How? By applying the principles of mentoring — Kingdom style.

One translation of the Bible interprets Jesus' words to the Twelve this way: "Anyone who intends to come with me has to let Me lead. You're not in the drivers seat; I am . . . self-sacrifice is the way, My way, to finding yourself, your true self."

Jesus wanted to plant His life into theirs. For nearly

three years He walked out the undeniable truth that character is more caught than taught. His goal, as He touched their lives, was to "grow" them into being a reflection of who He was.

What about Judas? Did the process fail with him? No. Emphatically, No!

Judas was chosen to betray the Saviour. Although I'm not a theologian, it was obvious from the comments Jesus made in the Upper Room and elsewhere that Judas was assigned for the purpose of betrayal.

There is another lesson we can learn from Jesus' experience with Judas, however. Potential mentors must remember that not everyone we spend time with and invest our lives in will always "catch" what we're hoping he or she will. There could conceivably be a Judas in our midst.

The apostle Paul said, "Follow (imitate) me as I follow Christ."

This is the mentor's role in the Kingdom. The mentor transfers — into the life of his follower — his life: who he is, his wisdom, his values, his ethics.

The Equipping Process

The exciting and effective method of mentoring is experiencing a revival in the church of the 1990s. The mentoring ninth wave assists the leadership of the church in the following areas:

> • Mentoring helps redirect our emphasis to people not problems.
> • Mentoring allows us to expand the opportunities for serving more people.

> • The mentoring concept is a logical next-step approach to an in-place discipleship plan.
> • Paul tells us to equip the saints; mentoring is an equipping procedure.

Mentoring, however, can take several forms.

Bob Shank, senior pastor of South Coast Community Church of Irvine, California, in a publication[1] from Fuller Institute, noted several varieties of mentoring :

1. Role mentoring

This type emphasizes the personal conduct of the protégé. Women in the church are a good example of this type of mentoring. (See Titus 2:4-5.)

Examples of role mentoring today include:
- Professionals in business
- Participants in marriage
- Players in sports

2. Soul mentoring

This method emphasizes character building. The relationship between Paul and Timothy is a good biblical example. (See 2 Tim. 1:1-7.)

Soul mentoring helps the student develop:
- Integrity
- Humility
- Accountability
- Other positive character traits

3. Whole mentoring

In this type, the personal calling into ministry is mentored into another individual. Using the example of Elijah and Elisha in Scripture, the transferable concept of the calling is emphasized. (See 1 Kings 19:15-21.)

Whole mentoring deals with these aspects:
• Understanding of their call
• Personal preparation
• Reasonable expectations

I've had the personal privilege of mentoring a number of young people in our ministry over the last 15 years who have later gone into full-time Christian service. Some are serving as youth pastors or senior pastors in growing churches around the country. There's hardly a greater thrill for a pastor than seeing young protégés launch out into their own ministry.

When we began our ministry, God explained to me that our church would become a teaching center where people could be trained and mentored for the ministry. It's an awesome responsibility, but one that carries a great reward.

God wants us to catch this "ninth wave" that is moving through His church. We can do that by putting a greater emphasis on the mentoring relationship and process of building Kingdom champions.

Too Busy for Individuals?

Julia Ward Howe, the social reformer, once asked Senator Charles Sumner to interest himself in the case of a person who needed some help.

The Senator answered: "Julia, I've become so busy I can no longer concern myself with individuals."

Julia replied, "Charles, that is quite remarkable. Even God hasn't reached that stage yet!"

Aren't you glad God is not too busy!

The first time I heard that story I was reminded that although the apostle Paul was busy tent making, preaching, teaching, traveling, and writing, he was not too busy to recruit a young man named Timothy.

Paul chose this young man to mentor and to tutor, building on the foundational faith that he had acquired through the family mentoring process laid by a mentoring-mom and grandmother. (See 2 Tim. 1:5.)

Ten Principles of Kingdom Mentoring

Let's see what we can learn about mentoring from Paul's relationship with Timothy as revealed through Philippians 2:19-23.

Timothy was tutored to care for the people.

Paul told the church that Timothy would "sincerely care for their sake." The care for believers was a character trait Paul himself possessed and which he desired to impart to his young protégé.

Paul and Timothy were "like-minded."

Another translation says they were of "kindred spirit." The relationship between the mentor and pupil should result in a bonding, a togetherness, a oneness, such as was the case with Paul and Timothy.

Timothy's character had been proven.

Paul points the Philippians to Timothy's "proven character." The true character of a person is never really known until it is proven in the arena of testing. Remember, character development and character-proving are a mentor's primary function.

Timothy is known as a servant.

Paul said Timothy served him — not as a mere "serving-servant" — but as a son serving his father. That's an important key in a Kingdom mentoring relationship. The tie is closer than just a one-on-one. It's deeper and more meaningful.

As a matter of fact, the deeper the relationship is allowed to grow, the greater the potential power the relationship will produce.

Paul had confidence in Timothy's abilities.

Paul so trusted his mentoree that Timothy was sent as a personal envoy of Paul's to check on the church at Philippi. Paul knew he had taught his young student well and that Timothy could be "cut loose" to carry on the tasks he had been trained to do.

Paul gave Timothy realistic counsel.

Timothy had been tutored to know what to expect in the field. As all good mentors should do, Paul told Timothy he would need to learn to "suffer hardship as a good soldier" (2 Tim. 2:3).

Paul instructed Timothy to stay focused.

Kingdom mentors teach their mentorees the need to be single-minded in their efforts whether in the ministry or the workplace. (See 2 Tim. 2:4.)

Coach Paul mentored Timothy in the concepts of self-discipline and the importance of ethics.

Paul loved athletics and used the example of athletic training to teach the principles of authentic Kingdom champions. (See 2 Tim. 2:5.)

Paul, by his words and example, communicated the work ethic to his young companion.

In other words, Timothy learned the meaning of hard work! We must tutor our students in the godly ethic of being not just busy, but productive in whatever our hands find to do. (See 2 Tim. 2:6.)

Paul encouraged Timothy to get involved in the mentoring process.

By taking what had been given to him and imparting those lessons to others, Timothy could continue the system by teaching others also. (See 2 Tim. 2:2.) Paul himself had been mentored by Barnabas, a wealthy real estate businessman who coached Paul in the early years of his ministry. (The story begins at Acts 9:27.) Now it was Timothy's turn to carry on the process.

This tenth principle takes us back full circle to the basis of mentoring that we discussed earlier:

> I do it, you watch.
> We do it together.
> You do it, I watch.
> I release you.
> You teach another, and so on, until the process of Kingdom mentoring ushers in the return of the Master mentor himself.

Chapter Nine

Hands
and Hearts

The Scriptures tell us that David shepherded the people with the integrity of his heart and the skillfulness of his hands.

Mentoring in the Kingdom and in the world is first a "heart" matter, then a "hands" matter.

One of the classic stories of a mentoring relationship is found in the Old Testament and involves the prophet Elijah and his servant.

Although not much is said about Elijah's servant, there are some things we can learn that might help us understand a significant truth regarding the blessings of a mentoring relationship.

We meet the unidentified servant for the first time in 1 Kings 18, after Elijah has successfully defeated the prophets of Baal on the Mountain of Carmel.

This nameless figure was with Elijah and must have beheld the great glory of God on Carmel, yet not much more is said of him. His role was disappointedly insignificant. As far as the Bible shows, the servant contributed nothing to the victory or to his master.

How Big Is God's Hand?

The servant remains with his master Elijah on the mount while the prophet prays for rain. The servant doesn't pray with Elijah and is simply told, "Go over there and watch the sky for signs of rain."

The servant goes and comes back with the report to Elijah, "There is nothing." Those three words say a lot about the character of this man.

Elijah sends him back again. Still the servant comes back with the same report. "There is nothing." His master has to send him back seven times!

Get the picture? Here is a prophet of faith, believing in fervent prayer for God to break the drought after 3 1/2 years. His servant, on the other hand, was a man who could see nothing by faith. He could not endure. He would not persevere. The words, "There is nothing," describe his low level of faith, faithfulness, and firmness!

Finally in verse 44, the seventh time the servant is sent to look, he comes back with the report ". . . a cloud as small as a man's hand is coming from the sea."

Not a cloud, mind you — a small cloud!

That adjective indicates a "small" faith. The servant obviously was surprised at seeing a cloud at all. He was impressed that it was small and obviously couldn't hold much water.

And, whose hand was the servant comparing the cloud to? A man's hand.

You see, Elijah was looking to God's hand for the blessing. See the difference?

Work the size of a man's hand doesn't accomplish much, but when God's hand reaches out to bless, there is the sound of abundance.

Elijah knew the floodgates of heaven were about to be opened up. The "little cloud" was God's handwriting in the sky. In Moses time, God's finger brought the Law; and later, God's handwriting on a wall brought judgment.

Elijah knew that God's finger is large enough to do damage to Satan's domain of darkness.

We know from reading verses 45 and 46 that the sky grew black with clouds, the wind blew, and there was heavy rain. God had answered in a big way!

It Could Have Been

Elijah now faced another problem.

In 1 Kings 19:3, we find Elijah full of fear and running for his life to escape the death threats of his arch-enemy, Jezebel. His servant runs with him.

It's not unusual for God's people to experience the power and abundance of the Lord's goodness and glory only to find ourselves, shortly thereafter, filled with fear and ruled by natural emotions. That's when a faithful companion can make all the difference. He can encourage us to trust in God and not look at the circumstances. But Elijah's servant offered no words of hope.

What happened to the prophet may have been averted had Elijah had another companion instead of his faithless servant.

When Elijah got to Beersheba, he "left his servant there." The partnership was dissolved as far as the prophet was concerned! That is the last mention of the servant.

Destiny had provided this servant-person a great opportunity to be mentored by Elijah. He could have, perhaps, been his successor.

Remember, however, this servant was Elijah's choice rather than God's.

Did this person turn away from serving God's man, considering the risk too high? Did he allow their relationship to come to an end because it was not what he was expecting? Was the association too hazardous?

Think again. It could have been *this* man-servant who witnessed the parting of the River Jordan. It could have been he who beheld Elijah's marvelous exit into Glory. It could have been he to whom was revealed a double-portion of Elijah's spirit. It could have been. But it wasn't.

The faithless servant missed it all and probably never realized what he had missed. When Elijah and he parted company, the servant simply passed into unrecorded oblivion.

The matter of who would succeed Elijah in his ministry was of utmost important. I believe it was important to Elijah, and I know it was important to God.

Having a successor was important enough to the prophet that he chose a person he hoped he could mentor into becoming the heir of God's anointing. Under fire, however, his choice was tested and found to be lacking.

One important truth all potential mentors in the Kingdom should realize: Loyalty, faithfulness, faith, commitment, and other positive attributes of a person's heart are never really known, until they are tested.

Elijah discovered something in the servant's life that caused him to realize that perhaps he had not made a wise choice. God had a man already picked who was to "wash the hands" of the prophet.

His name was Elisha. The man who was to receive a double-blessing as a result of a mentoring relationship with the prophet.

The Heart of an Elisha

Elijah was a man with a nature like ours. The Book of James tells us that. Perhaps that explains why Elijah found himself in such despair after experiencing supernatural victory over the prophets of Baal.

Nonetheless, in the midst of Elijah's depression, God speaks and commissions him to, among other things, choose Elisha to follow after him and to learn from him.

Key people are not always easy to find. In fact, they are so scarce only God knows who and where they are!

The Lord provided skilled people for Moses in order to build the tabernacle, and He brought forth labor-ers to do the work in building Solomon's Temple. After praying all night, the Father revealed to Jesus who His staff people were to be.

The Spirit of God will do the same for us.

There are people who are assigned to be Elishas in your life.

As we pick up the story in 1 Kings 19:20, we read: "Please let me [Elisha] kiss my father and mother, then I will follow you."

This is an important test for the would-be mentoree. Elijah was testing Elisha's willingness and eagerness to get involved in the relationship. Was he willing to pay the price? Would he be ready and willing to follow even in the midst of trial?

Here is the difference between the servant who missed much and the man Elisha.

Elisha had a heart for Elijah. He wanted to be like the prophet. He burned his bridges behind him, leaving what he had for what he could become.

A mentoree who profits much in a "coaching" relationship is willing to sacrifice what he is for what he can become. That's the heart of an Elisha.

Elisha faced a second test. Would he serve?

"Then he arose and followed Elijah and served him" (1 Kings 19:21).

Nothing had been said about the need for Elisha to serve. He simply already had the heart of a servant.

His apprenticeship did not consist of Elijah teaching him how to perform great miracles. His learning was based on his willingness to serve. He just wanted to be with this great man of God. He wanted to carry his briefcase, shine his shoes, fix his meals. He wanted to be the kind of man Elijah was, more than he wanted what he did!

If God chooses you to be mentored by a spiritual leader, be sure you have the heart of an Elisha before you commit yourself. Let's review the attitude that the mentoree is to bring into a mentoring relationship:

1. Make sure the appointment is God ordained.

2. Be willing to sacrifice what you are for what you can become.

3. Let go of anything that would detract you from your commitment. Forget what lies behind, press forward to what's ahead.

4. Purpose to develop a servant's heart in all you do. Humbling yourself puts you in a position to grow.

5. Want what your mentor is more than what he does.

No Near Misses

Arnold Palmer, without a doubt, is a legend in professional golf. His philosophy of life and competing was found in one simple but profound statement: "I wasn't going to lead a life of dear and near misses."

How many of us find ourselves content on just coming close? Like the man said, "That only counts in horseshoes."

Elisha was not going to miss what he believed God had for him, no matter what. He would not be denied.

We pick up the story of the dynamic-duo of the Old Testament in 2 Kings, chapter 2. We learn from verse 1 that Elijah went with Elisha from Gilgal, and in verse 2, Elijah tries to get Elisha to stay behind!

Elisha wouldn't think of it. He said "I will not leave you."

Let's think back to Elijah's never-to-be mentioned-again servant. He was left behind in Jezreel. (See 1 Kings 19:3.) Remember?

Note the difference between Elisha and him. This teaches us much about the relationship between the mentor and mentoree.

Elijah was putting Elisha to the test. Would he follow or stay behind and quit? Was he loyal to the relationship, or was he just in it for a short while?

You'll notice the same scene being played out twice more in verse 4 and again in verse 6. Elisha proved himself unbending in his willingness to follow through in his apprenticeship.

In verse 3 and again in verse 5, the sons of the prophets came out to Elisha and tried to tell him it was no use following Elijah anymore because his master was about to be taken away.

Elisha's response: "Yes I know; be still."

He would not allow anyone to talk badly about his coach. He would not allow others to talk him out of fulfilling what he had been called to do.

This is the kind of attitude we need to see lived in our local churches. We need people who refuse to murmur against one another or against leadership. If people wouldn't listen to gossip, people wouldn't talk!

Twice as Much

Elijah, in verse 9, tells his mentoree, "Ask what I should do for you before I'm taken from you."

How beautiful. These words reveal the heart of a mentor. He is always concerned about the student.

Remember, a true mentor is not a master but a servant himself. He sacrifices himself for the learner. He's willing to sacrifice his comfort and privacy. Remember, Jesus washed the feet of His staff.

A mentor unlocks the future of his apprentice and provides what he needs to achieve his own dream.

Elisha could have asked for a number of things from Elijah, but he asked for the indescribable gift that would bring to pass the change in his life he had always hoped for. Not a gift of things or "stuff." He wanted a double-portion of everything that Elijah was.

A double-portion of the Elijah attitude, anointing, perception, ability, and authority.

Elijah's answer explains why Elisha would never leave him. Listen to verse 10: "If you see me when I'm taken, it shall be so."

No wonder Elisha had not wanted to be out of his mentor's presence. He didn't want to risk being in the wrong place at the wrong time.

As Elijah was taken up in the whirlwind, his mantle fell from his shoulders at the feet of his protégé. Elisha took the mantle, struck the water as his master had done, and cried out with a loud voice, "Where is the Lord, the God of Elijah?" And the waters divided!

So the ministry of Elisha began — a ministry that

reflected the character and the heart of his departed master. The story of Elisha tells us he performed twice as many miracles as did his "father" Elijah.

The sons of the prophets watched Elisha and exclaimed, "The Spirit of Elijah rests on Elisha." The mentoree reflected his coach.

Later, when Jehoshaphat asked for a prophet it was said, "Elisha . . . is here, who used to serve Elijah." What an awesome testimony.

That's what Kingdom mentoring is all about.

Chapter Ten

Worthy of Duplication?

I've had the privilege through the years to meet many people who were impacting lives in a significant way by their willingness to share what God had done in them to others who were hungry to grow.

One such couple came into my life about three years ago. Dony McGuire and Reba Rambo (McGuire) have an understanding of the "Master's Mentoring Mentality" about as well as anyone.

Let me share their story with you.

Dony and Reba experienced a miracle restoration of their marriage and ministry in the early 1980s. God put their lives and hearts back together in a magnificent way.

Dony explains what followed:

One of the first words that I can remember God speaking to us during the restoration process was this: "The true mark of success in My kingdom is the raising-up of successors."

With that word in our hearts, not even fully understanding all that it meant, this incredible journey began.

Since we had never given of ourselves in this manner before, we didn't know what to expect. God put a desire in us to pour out of ourselves and to share our platform of ministry with others. We felt that this kind of hands-on training would enable us not only to cultivate and develop the talents and gifts of those God brought us, but to give of ourselves in a daily impartation.

The responsibility is much greater when you move someone into your home, but this was the best way we knew to obey the Lord.

Dony and Reba's first mentoring experience happened when they became aware of a young black lady with a child out of wedlock. God directed them to open their home to this mother and child.

For nearly two years they lived with Dony and Reba, traveled with them, ate with them, and were always together.

Dony says, "We didn't just give her a bunch of teaching tapes and videos or spiritual books to read, but rather it was through the experiences we encountered together that the mother, Patty, began to grow."

Patty eventually was able to rise above the circumstances of her past and was ready to begin a whole new life. Patty is now ministering the light of God through her music in dark places where Dony and Reba could never go.

A Training Camp on Wheels

After Patty, a seemingly endless string of young people came to the McGuires from the homes of ministers. These were kids who could no longer relate to their parents for one reason or another. Some were cocaine addicts, young girls who had been molested by their fathers, and kids whose parents were simply no longer able to cope with the pressures of ministry and raise their children, too.

During this season the McGuire house seemed more like a hospital than a home.

Dony does add, however, that out of the young people who came to them devastated, all but one have returned to their places of residence, some are now married with children, and some are even in positions of ministry!

The years of greatest challenge for these new Kingdom mentors were 1987 and 1988, and God taught them many things through the situations they encountered.

Dony points out, "Some of those God brought our way were not devastated at all, but merely in need of a push in the right direction toward their destiny in God. All that we could do was to live a life before them that allowed them to see the person of Christ in us."

A further revelation of the Rambo/McGuire

mentoring purpose came through an understanding of Luke 6:40.

Dony paraphrases:

A student isn't above his teacher, and a perfectly trained student will be just like his teacher!

Dony was challenged with that word. "Were we worthy of duplication? If they get all that we can teach them, the best we can hope for — outside of God's intervention — is that they be like us. That understanding causes us to press on toward the mark of maturity and fullness in Christ."

The more Dony and Reba understood their purpose in raising up successors, the more the vision seemed to expand.

In May of 1992 God spoke to them about those they had poured their lives into over the past decade.

The Lord said, "It won't take you a decade to raise up the next eight ministry gifts, but rather pursue raising up eight ministers per year. Prepare a bus with eight places, and a musical work station to further cultivate these gifts — prepare a training camp on wheels!"

Dony says, "I'll not soon forget the next words that came out of my mouth — 'We can't do that God!' "

But the Lord assured Dony that He would not instruct them to do simply what *they* could do.

Dony adds:

**Our dependence upon Him is insured by
the overwhelming size of the tasks He
gives us!**

Do You Do Bathrooms?

As the Rambo/McGuire team shares their vision
with people around the country, they're literally bom-
barded with requests from pastors, parents, and kids
alike, to become a part of this mentoring and disciplining program.

Both Dony and Reba considered the necessary
guidelines and parameters that God would have them
place around their mentorees. Not surprisingly, many
disqualified themselves early-on.

For example, the first question asked of these potential protégés is, "Who is your pastor?"

Dony says: "I'm overwhelmed by the number of
people who somehow expect to be used in God's kingdom but who have absolutely no sense of connection
to eldership."

Question number two disqualifies as many as number one. Dony asks, "Will your pastor vouch for your
faithfulness in the local church for the past 12 months?
Have you been faithful in the choir? Have you been
faithful over the little assignments? Have you been
faithful to your Youth Department? Have you been
faithful in your covenant over His tithe and your offer-
ing? Are you faithful to show up for special work days?
Are you submissive to those God has placed over you

and your gifts? Can your pastor attest to the worldwide potential for your ministry-gift?"

Few make it through this kind of query, but if they do, and they board the "training camp on wheels" (not to be mistaken for a "reform school on wheels"), they are given their first assignment. Handed a roll of paper towels and a bottle of 409 cleanser, they are pointed in the direction of the bathrooms.

Reba points out, "Shock waves have been seen to attack many as the words, 'I don't *do* bathrooms' form on their lips. If that attitude is truly in their hearts, then they also don't *do* training camp."

Both Dony and Reba understand that Jesus said greatness comes through servanthood. They both realize if a person is not willing to serve, then that person has little hope for greatness in His kingdom. If a person won't humble himself, the Lord will not lift him up.

Dony makes this point: "I have found the greatest release of the life of Christ in me comes as I am preferring others ahead of myself and serving as Christ did. I hope that this example is demonstrated properly to those God brings us."

Iron Sharpening Iron

To assist us in the mentor process, books, tapes, videos, and anything else that will help to equip people for the work of the ministry are used in the mobile training camp.

Both Dony and Reba feel deeply about this unique ministry God has given them. They point out: "Since iron sharpens iron, we've had the delightful experience of becoming more disciplined in our own craft because these young people keep us on our toes! Their energy and enthusiasm is contagious! This creative environment of youthful zeal, coupled with age and experience, has produced, and is producing, such bountiful fruit for the Kingdom. We are constantly amazed at how quickly these young gifts develop while in this intense training program."

Dony recognizes that one of their primary purposes is to focus each student toward their divine destiny. By presenting "the big picture" of God's redemptive plan, these young people come to see their role as kings and priests in the household of faith.

Another part of the mentoring process is the confrontation that must be faced when questioned by these young people. Reba says: "They can't be fooled or put off. Sometimes we have to frankly respond with an 'I don't know.' As a matter of fact, there are times when we wonder who is doing the teaching because we truly do learn from them! In this atmosphere of mutual trust, learning, love, and acceptance there are endless possibilities for growth."

While participating in the "rolling" mentoring relationship, the young people are also strongly encouraged to pursue furthering their education through college, Bible school, workshops, books, tapes, etc. Everyone in the training camp, however, recognizes some things can only be learned from experience.

After almost every church service where the kids give testimonies or sing, each of the mentorees are asked, "What did you learn tonight?" They are then given a chance to express what they learned and its significance in their life.

"We are praying about the possibility of a permanent school in Nashville to supplement what we do on the road because so many people need mentoring," says Dony.

In summary, Dony states, "We believe that the anointing flows out of an obedient lifestyle. We further believe that the anointing is 'caught' as much as taught."

Dony realizes that God also wants to work in his and Reba's lives. "This process of raising up and training others has certainly pressed us," he says. "Hopefully it will press us to 'death.' "

Why does he say that? Because one of the first Scriptures they share with their students is Galatians 2:20, which says, "Having considered that I have died, I now enjoy a second existence, which is simply . . . Jesus, using my body.' "

Any mentor who has that kind of attitude is certainly worthy of duplication.

How about you?

Chapter Eleven

Identifying True Leaders

"Nothing great is done without great men," Charles de Gaulle wrote, "and these are great because they willed it so."

In Kingdom leadership another truth stands out: "Nothing great is done without men who will to serve a great God."

It is often said that a leader motivates the masses. The mentor, however, molds the few. At the same time, leadership and mentoring have strong ties that fit the two skills closely together.

To assist us in broadening our concepts of the mentor-novice relationship, we need to examine the qualities and characteristics of leaders.

"What is the most important characteristic a successful leader must have?" asks Richard Nixon in his book, *Leaders.* He goes on to tell us there is no single answer.

"Leadership is the enthusiasm to motivate others" — *E.M. Estes.*

Nixon does, however, list certain qualities he has discovered in leaders around the world that will give us some degree of insight. The former president suggests high intelligence, courage, hard work, tenacity, judgment, dedication to a great cause, and a "certain measure of charm."

Other ingredients that Mr. Nixon itemizes include the ability to out-work, out-think, and out-fight the opposition. He further states the leader needs insight, foresight, and the willingness to take the bold but calculated risk. Above all the leader must be decisive and must not succumb to "paralysis by analysis."[1]

The Greatest Leader of All

When we discuss leadership traits, skills, and characteristics, we must include those possessed by the greatest leader who ever walked the earth — Jesus of Nazareth!

The Master's leadership examples and teaching should be our platform to understand what true Kingdom-style leading encompasses. Let's examine the leadership principles He taught us as He motivated and moved masses to an awareness of what it means to be a Kingdom champion.

Servants become leaders. Jesus taught that servanthood was a prerequisite to becoming a leader. (See Matt. 20:20-28.) God creates servants not leaders. True leaders are guided by the human needs they come to serve, just as Jesus was.

Leaders are followers. They are under authority. In Matthew 8:5-13, the Roman centurion (a leader) recognizes Jesus' submission to His authority. Kingdom leadership must serve a higher purpose. A purpose higher than the potential stature of the leader. He must be submissive to a greater call.

Kingdom leaders have a strong sense of purpose. They know what needs to be done and how to accomplish it. "I have come down from heaven not to do my will, but the will of Him who sent me," Jesus declared in John 6:38. In another place He said, "My will is to do the will of Him who sent me and to finish His work" (John 4:34).

Kingdom leaders attract others. You're not a leader because of your position. You're a leader because people follow you. Wherever Jesus went He attracted followers. The Twelve, however, He chose to mentor. The multitudes He led.

Leaders never lord over those entrusted to their charge. Jesus was a dealer in hope. He lifted people up. He never talked down to anyone. Even those who would oppose Him He treated with a quiet strength that left no doubt of His position. (See John 8.) He was uncommon as to whom He was, but He was common in His availability.

The Kingdom leader knows not only how to talk, but also how to listen. Jesus amazed with His words, and in His quietness He retained control. When people talked to Him, Jesus listened to more than their words — He listened to their heart.

Authentic Kingdom leadership knows when to be the aggressor and when to back off. Jesus cleansed the temple not once but twice. Yet in Luke 4, He quietly passes through the crowd that tries unsuccessfully to throw Him from the mount. He knew when to take the offensive and when to just fade away.

Effective and efficient leaders know how, when, and to whom to delegate authority and responsibility. Jesus did. In Luke 9:1-2, He gave His Twelve power and authority. In the tenth chapter, He appointed 70 others and sent them out. Leaders recognize that delegation means you stop doing other people's work. Delegation does not mean you get them to do yours.

Leaders think ahead and know when to act. Jesus taught the principles of leadership and thought and action. Too often the man of thought cannot act and the man of action cannot think. Jesus, of course, encompasses both qualities. He was the creative thinker as well as the decisive man of action.

Leaders are learners. In Luke 2:40-52 we learn another truth regarding true leaders. Jesus amazed the scholars of His day with His great learning. Even as a young man He was found sitting "in the midst of teachers." Today authentic leadership stays informed. The true leader reads, studies, develops new skills, and seeks to sharpen old ones.

Leaders establish human relationships based on

trust, respect, caring, and love. Jesus mentored the Twelve, but had a special relationship with Peter, James, and John. Also His relationship with Lazarus and his sisters was most unique. There was a mutual commitment, care, and love in all of His relationships.

Great leaders often spark great controversies. Jesus was unwavering in His purpose and calling. Unbending in principle, He refused to compromise truth. Needless to say, His life, His mission, and His words created controversy among the religious people of the day.

Leaders attract and live with opposition. No other leader from any other period in time can hold a candle to the opposition Jesus encountered. Religious rulers, even one from His own ranks, moved in direct opposition to His ministry. He understood that there would always be opposition to His mission and purpose.

Authentic leaders are powerfully persistent. They endure in the face of insurmountable obstacles. They persevere when everyone around them is ready to wave the white flag of surrender. Jesus exemplified staying power when all others would leave Him, forsake Him, deny Him, and even betray Him. (See John 6:15 and Mark 9:5.)

If you desire to increase your leadership skills, study the Master's leadership touch. Develop it and release it in your life.

The characteristics we've listed here are only a few of the qualities that Jesus taught us regarding what a leader is and does. The list goes on and on. Make your own list. Then adapt the principles into your life.

Developing Leadership in Others

"Pastor, I'm looking for a mentor!"

The young woman speaking to me after a mid-week service was eagerly seeking my counsel as to which of the older women of the church might be willing to spend time with her. Her goal: to be all that God wanted her to be.

"Pastor, the Word says the older women are to teach the younger. I want that. Not another Bible study, but a relationship. I want to receive in my life the anointing that is on the life of a truly reverent woman of God."

It was my pleasure to assist this young lady in becoming involved with an older lady in our congregation who had served as an evangelist for a number of years. The anointing and spiritual wisdom in the life of this proven vessel was exactly what this young woman needed.

How did I know? Because Titus 2:3-5 makes the basis for such a relationship quite clear:

> The older women likewise, that they by reverent in behavior, not slanderers, not given to much wine, teachers of good things — that they admonish the young women to love their husbands, to love their children, to be discreet, chaste, homemakers, good, obedient to their own husbands, that the word of God may not be blasphemed.

What should a new mentoree look for in a mentor? How does the mentoree know whether she is being mentored or counseled or discipled or what? Format and style vary depending upon the people involved.

"It's different every time," says Terrie Pergason of Clovin, California, mentor and author of *"Designed to Disciple: The Mentor's Role in Developing Leadership."*[2]

Terrie says her goal is to help her pupils "figure out where they want to go then help them get there."

The goals of the mentor may be consistent with each person, but the steps or procedures getting there will vary depending upon the needs of the "mentoree."

Studying a book together; testing to determine certain gifts; casual conversations regarding the daily routine of living; or facing the challenges of life — these are all mentoring styles or procedures (plus many others) that will be effective.

Finding a Kingdom Mentor

Those who choose a mentor must first look for someone they can trust. It should be someone who operates from a heart of love and not a position of power.

A word of warning. Whether in the workplace or the church, there are those who want to control and manipulate others. Some people find their source of power in causing novices to develop a co-dependent relationship with them. Avoid these kinds of people.

In the church environment, especially, we should exercise extreme caution in not allowing a mentoring relationship to steer us into false teaching or doctrine. I have personally witnessed the devastating effects of such relationships. Be on the alert.

A God-inspired mentor will always allow you to follow after the Lord in freedom. The mentor will never put you in bondage to them or a philosophy. Remember, a mentor models their relationship with the Word and with God. They are not in your life to coerce you. Follow them as they follow Christ.

What should you do to find a Kingdom mentor for your life? Let me give you some suggestions:

Pray

Ask God to send you or bring into your life the person best suited (according to His will) to function in that role.

Ask

Go to your pastor and ask him to recommend someone with whom you might establish a mentoring relationship.

Be Patient

Wait for the Lord to act. Don't push. His timing and will are perfect.

Be Expectant

Be sensitive to the people around you. God may have your mentor sitting beside you in the next church service!

Confirm Your Choice

When you think you have discovered your mentor, check it out with your pastor or some other spiritual advisor. God will use others to confirm if your decision is right. Remember, in the multitude of counselors there is safety.

Mentoring or Discipleship?

The Fall 1993 issue of *Virtue Magazine*, a publication directed primarily at Christian women, ran a rather lengthy article devoted to women mentoring women. Several interesting insights are given.

For example, the article highlights the difference between mentoring and discipleship. The distinction is made by pointing out that discipleship teaches the how-to's of spiritual growth while mentoring focuses more on nurturing.

It is noted that while discipleship is perhaps more structured, mentoring is more open-ended. Mentors don't give all the answers; they're too busy listening for the questions and looking farther down the road for what their mentoree needs.

There are many similarities between these two functions in the Church, and to be able to distinguish between discipleship and mentoring is not easy.

Some define mentoring as a deliberate impartation of wisdom from one to another in areas that are more defined as "secular," such as how to become a better employee or manager. Timely subjects such as more effective "fathering or mothering" are often dealt with in a mentoring/nurturing relationship. Ethics and value systems are all-inclusive in mentoring.

Discipleship deals with the more spiritual aspects

of our Christianity. The how-to's of Bible reading and study, prayer, and worship are all subjects covered in a discipling process.

At the risk of over-simplification, discipling deals more with transfer of knowledge whereas mentoring concentrates on the application of that knowledge, commonly considered as "wisdom."

Both the mentor and/or the disciple use God's Word as a basis for the counsel, and both depend deeply on the guidance of the Spirit.

We might also add that mentoring is considered by many to be less structured than traditional discipling. The mentor doesn't try to give all the answers or solve all the problems his protégé may be facing, but instead, challenges the learner to seek answers on his own.

The mentoree is kept focused on the big picture instead of the immediacy of the relationship. The mentor constantly asks where the mentoree is going to be in his life tomorrow, next month, or next year.

Methods vary from person to person, and the results are based on the special needs of the mentoree. One thing, however, is standard: The ultimate objective of any Kingdom discipleship or mentoring relationship should be authentic Christianity. With that as the final goal, how can anyone lose?

Chapter Twelve

Setting the Standard

Helen was nearly paralyzed with fear by rumors of impending layoffs. She was employed by a hospital in a northeastern state, and rumor of the cutbacks began to circulate shortly after she began her job there.

A decade later, the layoffs actually came. Helen's fears had come to pass.

After nearly two years of sending out scores of resumes and applications, she found a job working with the disabled. Now, Helen says, old fears have disappeared as she learned during her unemployment to place "ultimate faith" in God.

Joseph Gosse, author of a booklet, *Unemployed Workers,* [1] points out that many unemployed people he interviewed spoke of a deepened spirituality as a result of their trial. Some reported returning to the faith they had known as a child growing up.

In a recent Associated Press article, Joseph Belechak, an unemployment counselor is quoted as saying: "I'm finding more and more unemployed people whose attachment to God is becoming much stronger."

Like most trials, being out of work makes us much more dependent on God. After exhausting all their own attempts and resources, the unemployed worker eventually realizes that without a miracle, finding the kind of job he or she wants is next to impossible.

The church must be relevant in addressing real needs of real people. Many business people tend to feel that the clergy are either biased against business or ignorant of its realities. People are searching for ways to integrate their faith into their everyday work life.

Here are some things churches can do to let the work force know they're interested in helping them deal with everyday issues in the marketplace.

1. The church should drill the work ethic into the lives of its people.

Pastors would do well to research the work ethics that have their roots in the Scriptures, and then pass them on to their congregations. For example, Colossians 3:22-4:1 contains some very practical insights into this issue.

Teach the concepts that employers are looking for in their employees.

- Adherence to company policies denotes faithfulness on the part of an employee.
- Integrity and sincerity in service to our bosses and employers is a must.
- Hearty effort should be put forth in our labor, bearing in mind Ecclesiastes 9:10, "Whatever your hand finds to do, do it with all your might."
- Develop a reputation of diligence.
- Pursue quality work in an effort to please the Lord.
- Trust God to provide ability to perform your tasks.
- Employ management ethics which include not showing partiality, but using just and fair policies in managing employees.

2. The church should assist in teaching the importance of discovering their vocation.

Frequently, our frustration with life is found in being in a vocation that is not fulfilling. We're simply working to be working.

The Bible tells us that we are to enjoy the good of all our labor, for it is our heritage. (See Eccles. 5:18.)

The Chinese have a proverb that states: "If a man has a job he loves, he'll never have to work a day in his life."

The church can offer assistance as to where to find job counseling professionals. There are aptitude and personality testing facilities where members of the congregation can find job selection assistance.

The church should be bold in job referrals. Most of the people sitting in our churches are spending at least a third of their life in the work force — let's talk about how they can enjoy that part of their lives even more.

3. The church should be a motivating force that teaches the principles of self-responsibility.

"If a man doesn't work, neither shall he eat" (2 Thess. 3:10).

I recently talked with the general manager of a very successful company who was explaining why he had to let a particular employee go.

The person, he said, would not accept responbility for their lack of performance. When I questioned the manager about the particulars, he explained that the former employee was continually blaming other co-workers, circumstances, or the company for his problems. The manager further indicated the issue really was grounded in the fact the ex-worker had a major attitude problem.

Incidentally, the worker is a Christian — very vocal about their Christianity, but obviously unwilling or ignorant in how to apply the basic principles of authentic Christian living in the market place.

In our church I have used a number of sermons to teach the following attitudes necessary to achieve in our job:

- The biggest mistake in your life is to believe you work for someone else.

- There is no future in any job; your future is in your attitude.
- The highest reward for our labor is not what we get for it, but what we become by it.

This is just a partial list, obviously. But the point is, we have a responsibility as a church to be a motivating force in the lives of our people regarding the subject of everyday living.

4. The church should instruct its people in relevant skills.

These should be skills that can be applied Monday morning at the plant or office, such as:

- Human relations ("Sermon on the Mount" principles),
- Excellence (the Book of Proverbs),
- Attitudes (the Book of Proverbs),
- Management and leadership (the life of Jesus),
- Overcoming stress, discouragement, fear, etc. (the Epistles),
- Principles of achievement (the lives of David, Nehemiah, and others).

5. The church should provide a support system for unemployed workers.

This can be done by helping the unemployed develop resumes, providing counseling and prayer partners, and assisting with temporary financial needs.

Turning Things Around

A recent Harris poll found some surprising statistics:

> • 63 percent of workers polled believed that very few people work as hard as they did 10 years ago.
> • 78 percent said workers today take less pride in their work than they did 10 years ago.
> • 69 percent thought workmanship in America today has become inferior to what it was 10 years ago.
> • 73 percent believed that workers are less motivated today then they were 10 years ago.[2]

These findings shouldn't surprise anybody.

Nor should it surprise you that America is alone among the industrialized nations of the world to *decrease* its industrial output over the last 10 years — *the only one!*

In another poll, only 16 percent responding said they were doing the best job they could at work, and 84 percent said they could do better and work harder. Many said they could even be twice as effective if they wished.

Why do people feel this way?

Because discontentment with one's own performance equals a morale crisis. As a result, dispirited and discouraged workers create a downward spiral in productivity.

Another poll said 88 percent of the workers found

that working hard and doing their best was very important.

What is happening?

If working hard is important to 88 percent of the people, then why aren't they doing it?

I'll tell you why.

The next figure explains it all. It seems that 84 percent of the people said they would work harder and would do their best if they could gain something for it!

That explains why they aren't giving their all. *They have no incentive to excel!* They are paid the same whether they do a magnificent job or a mediocre one.

If a person has a heavy workload, pure old human laziness is apt to kick in. Why work 60 hours a week, sacrificing time with the kids or on the golf course, if the pay is the same for 40 hours?

I don't know about you, but this kind of talk makes me uneasy. It makes me concerned about where our nation is headed.

Don't get me wrong. I am not a prophet of doom. I don't want to be accused of running around like Henny Penny clucking that "the sky is falling, the sky is falling."

If I didn't feel that I had an answer, I might be alarmed. But I believe we have a solution that will not only turn your life around, but that will revolutionize the way we all do business. In fact, I believe it could turn things around in America!

What could?

Mentoring.

The "Can-Do" Attitude

John Havlicek is a champion. As a Boston Celtic, he was known as "Mr. Perpetual Motion." Once Havlicek started running he didn't stop for 16 seasons. Havlicek always gave 100 percent effort. Hustle alone would have cloaked him with the mantle of great basketball stars. But to that he added production, leadership, and performance.

John Havlicek was the standard by which other basketball players were measured. He was the very soul of the sports expression "He came to play."

We know the "he came to play" attitude wins in athletics, but it's also true in the work force.

Christians should be the standard of measure by which other workers are measured in the marketplace. They should be the ones displaying the "can-do" attitude.

The traditional American work ethic is a "can-do" attitude. It is the desire to work as hard as necessary to do a top-notch job, then to reap the benefits, not only financially, but in satisfaction of individual fulfillment and personal prestige and advancement.

In the book *Why American Doesn't Work,* by Chuck Colson, Dorothy Sayers is quoted as saying:

In nothing has the church so lost her hold on reality as in her failure to understand and respect our secular vocation.

Sayers points out that the church should tell a carpenter to stop getting drunk and come to church on Sunday. But, Sayers continues, the church should also be telling him that "the very first demand that religion makes on him is that he should make good tables."

She goes on to ask: "What use was his piety in church attendance if he was insulting God with bad carpentry?"[3]

This is where mentoring in the church can be so relevant. Not just in the development of new or traditional church leadership but in helping today's Christian work force make an impact in the world.

Jungle Tactics

As I travel and speak at secular as well as Christian-based meetings, I hear the same thing over and over again: "I don't need another theological sermon. I need to know how to make it through another week."

Like a frazzled Tarzan said to Jane as he came home from another hard day swinging through the trees: "Whew, it's a jungle out there!"

Hey, Church, the Tarzans of our congregation really need our help!

Some churches are making mentoring programs available to their people to assist them in reflecting the excellence of the work ethic in their lives.

At our church we began a "Men's Mentoring Group" that meets every other week. As a former businessman, I know at least some of the issues confronting Christians in the work force, at home, and in everyday living. That's why the mentoring group has had such widespread acceptance among the men in our church.

In this mentoring group, teenagers and older retired executives sit side by side. Corporate officers, physicians, and common laborers are together to learn. It's a great group of eager-to-grow champions.

In the group we discuss men's roles in family leadership, spiritual gifts, and how to be more effective in our everyday work. We have outside teachers from the business community address the group. All in all, we want these men to know there are real answers to everyday situations.

Also, once a month on a Sunday morning, I do another teaching from a series called "The Career Development Series." These teachings deal with such topics as: "How to Climb the Ladder of Promotion and Pay Raises;" "More Effective Communication Skills;" "What Does Today's Employer Look For in an Employee?" "How to be a Better Manager;" etc.

The response from these teachings has been exciting.

A local businessman remarked recently: "The practical, relevant teachings I receive here at church would cost me thousands of dollars in seminar fees. It's so good to know these relevant issues are addressed here."

I believe that's what church is all about.

Part 4

*Mentoring
in the
Marketplace*

Chapter Thirteen

Buying into Another's Dream

For a number of years my business career involved "playing second fiddle." Whether as an assistant to the manager or executive vice president to the president, I spent nearly 15 years as the number two man at some level on the corporate organizational chart.

These years were a time of preparation. I was being readied for the day I could move into the "top" spot.

During this time, I allowed myself to be mentored. I understood that I could submit to learning and increase knowledge — or grumble. Because I wanted my big chance, I chose to submit to mentors who were there to assist me in fulfilling my dream.

"True mentoring is a process by which you buy into another's dream," says Ben Borne, a Chicago-based human resources consultant.

"You help the people you mentor achieve professional goals by sharing your experience and wisdom," he says. "It is dynamic partnering that benefits all the participants."

I believe the number one responsibility a mentor has to their mentoree is to assist in character building. It is important that skills and abilities and job counseling be a part of the mentoring sessions, but first and foremost, the mentor/pupil relationship is geared to seeing positive character traits established.

Not every mentor brought into your life will be exactly what you might be hoping for. Some can be your greatest tormentors!

Yet even in that type of a relationship you can gain and grow and prosper — if you choose to.

Crisis is not the developer of character, but the greatest revealer of character.

It is estimated that a third of the nation's major companies now have a formal mentoring program.

Most business experts agree that companies who are reluctant to initiate mentoring programs are missing out on implementing ideas, talent, and savings.

Better Than a Seminar

A small Vancouver, Canada, based company called Pathfinder Software had only eight employees when they adopted their mentor program.

Pathfinder's problem, according to mentoring consultant William A. Gray, who designed its mentor program, was how to train its people to use "PowerHouse," a new programming language, without sending them to an expensive seminar.

Since the company was small, the management wanted every employee — no matter what his or her assigned job — to be able to help sell the company's products. To do that, every person had to become a "universalist" in the small company's world.

How could that be accomplished? Through mentoring.

Gray taught the company's employees how to teach their expertise (marketing, sales, production, etc.) to one another, and as they came aboard, to new hirees. For example, the company's salesperson taught everyone how a sale should be conducted.

The employees learned faster from each other than they would have at seminars, Gray says. In fact, the new project managers who were developed through mentoring were better at estimating and controlling company costs.

In addition, Gray says, "The teaching and coaching skills the mentors learned to use with protégés were also employed when teaching [the company's] clients to use software systems, greatly reducing the number of call-backs Pathfinder had to 'hand-hold' the clients through the process of learning the system."

Writing in *Mentoring International*, a periodical he also edits, Gray notes that Pathfinder gained enough new clients after instituting mentoring to double the number of its employees.

Avoiding the Pitfalls

Companies that set up a mentoring program need to be wary of the pitfalls involved, however. To avoid these problems, keep these rules in mind:

Design the program so that the protégés have more than one mentor.

This ensures that they get the benefit of several individuals' advice and support. In addition, having just one mentor puts the mentoree in danger of becoming an "orphan" should the mentor leave the company.

Don't try to create a program in troubled waters.

Mentor relationships are sensitive and often psychologically based. The pressures of, say, a business crisis will put these relationships at risk if for no other reason than the senior managers are distracted.

Make it possible for employees to build mentor-like relationships with their peers.

These relationships should be between people who face the same kind of work challenges on a daily basis, such as learning the culture or gaining visibility. Example: Salesperson A tells Salesperson B, who is having trouble routing calls efficiently, that he learned to do it by scheduling the most promising calls first to create a "winning" attitude for the day.

Be careful that mentors do not develop such a dependency on their protégés that the latter, in fact, become their assistants.

The mentoree should be treated as a professional at all times by the mentor.

Don't treat your protégés as special or privileged people, even when they are.

No one benefits if a "class mentality" is allowed to develop among employees.

Why Mentoring Works

This article appeared in a 1993 edition of *USA Today*:

FEMALE EXECUTIVE MENTORS: About 15,000 women were urged to be mentors last weekend in a satellite town meeting sponsored by the National Association for Female Executives. The event was billed as the largest meeting of women ever held in the USA — linking 100 sites across the nation. Participants agreed mentoring will help young women and minorities reach NAFE's goal: "50/50 by 2000," or equal pay with men.

Everywhere we look more emphasis is placed on the mentoring approach to business and professional development. Why? Because it works!

People are being planted, watered, grown, and nurtured into fruitful employees because of this age-old system of assisting others to achieve the potential that is in them.

Jean Driscoll, a mentoring advocate, points to the five benefits a mentoring relationship can have in the life of the mentoree:

1. Career planning
2. Leadership development
3. Professional advancement
4. Increased creativity
5. Increased courage for risk-taking

As a corporate executive, consultant, and more recently a pastor, I have counseled many people in career development. In doing so, I've discovered several stumbling blocks that keep workers frustrated in their jobs.

Let's examine some of those stumbling blocks in light of Ms. Driscoll's "Five Benefits of a Mentor" referred to above.

Career Planning

I recently read that 19 percent of men say if they could change one aspect of their lives it would be their careers. A mentor can help us make some wise discoveries relative to our career before it's too late.

Through their guidance we can enter into serious self-evaluation. We can check out our gifts and discover latent talents and abilities. Then the mentor can instruct us in the way to prepare, then plan, and execute the plan. Their objective counseling can help us steer clear of many career pitfalls.

Leadership Development

Many people are frustrated by their lack of growth process in the workplace because they think they should be advancing to positions of leadership more rapidly.

The mentor can assist in developing the mentoree's leadership skills and provide guidance regarding the importance of timing in the protégé's career.

The mentor also recognizes there is one time-honored error made by more companies regarding promotions than perhaps any other: An employee who does his work with great skills, ability, and excellence is automatically considered to be a good manager. This is not always true and can, in fact, frustrate both the ill-prepared employee and those under his or her supervision.

Professional Advancement

Advancement in the marketplace does not come just by my desire to progress up the ladder of promotion. Preparation is the key.

The mentor can provide continuing education suggestions, for example, which are a part of the preparation stage in a mentoree's life. Self-helps and extracurricular professional pursuits are a part of the mentor's guidance for their student, also.

The mentor and pupil recognize outer performance is a reflection of inner preparation.

Increased Creativity.

One asset every organization looks for in their human resource "bank" is creativity.

A mentoring relationship stimulates creative exploration. The mentoree has a support for adventuresome thinking. Hence, in a relationship between guide and protégé, the juices of dormant creativity are encouraged to flow.

Sam Walton, founder of Wal-Mart, had a personal philosophy of constantly encouraging his employees to a new level of creative thinking. It worked for Wal-Mart. It will work for you.

Increased Courage for Risk-Taking.

Too frequently we become so security conscious that we develop a fear of risk-taking.

Mentors can help in this area, too. They, as a friend or sponsor, provide a positive foundation from which the mentoree can launch out to challenge the status quo.

The wise mentor-coach will motivate us to develop the heart to move out of our comfort zone. They'll help us to muster the courage to crucify the seven last words of mediocrity and stagnation: "We never tried it that way before."

The undisciplined is a headache to himself and a heartache to others. He is unprepared to face the harsh realities of life.

In an Ohio State University study on mentoring, Lucy Sibley, chairwoman of the Department of Textiles and Clothing, supervised and co-authored a study by LuAnn Ricketts Gaskill of 205 female executives in textile apparel retailing, some of whom had mentors within their own companies.

"What Gaskill found," Sibley says, "was that mentored executives were promoted an average of 2.3 times in a five-year period, unmentored executives only 1.8 times.

"She also found that the upper-level executives had higher levels of job satisfaction and job motivation than did the non-mentored upper-level executives. In other words, women who are mentored and move up, especially when they get into that upper-level, tend to feel better about their jobs."

With benefits like these, mentoring in the marketplace certainly sounds appealing. As Christians, however, we need to choose our career mentors carefully.

Remember, character is always the one characteristic that will determine the quality and value of the mentoring relationship. Don't settle for less than the best.

Chapter Fourteen

Your Job Has No Future

In my years of business experience, I realized that I needed help if I was to achieve my dream. As a radio and TV personality for a number of years, I learned that everything I needed to know about broadcasting was not taught in my university broadcast school.

It was a rude awakening, but that discovery led me to another. I needed a mentor. Someone who would take the time to nurture me so that I would not humiliate myself each time I got on the air — someone who would help me grow in my career.

The good news is, I found that person.

Jim was an "old hand" in radio and TV. He knew the ropes. Most of all, he had a heart to help neophytes like me. That's what made him the perfect mentor.

Mentoring is a heart-to-heart relationship that is deeper than just a teacher-student tutoring arrangement.

Jim started out by giving me "air-checks." He would tape record portions of my on-the-air work and then go over the tapes with me, making suggestions designed to improve the quality of my broadcasting skills.

What a humbling experience that was! He would listen to what I said on the air, then he would show me the "better way." Jim shared with me his vast experience and wisdom, and taught me the things they didn't teach in school — and still don't, even to this day.

I guess Jim also saw the potential in me because he was committed to our relationship. He would stay late to help me and even worked with me on his day off. Whatever he could do to encourage me, he would do.

Jim was instrumental in drawing out of me a character trait that my parents had instilled in me while I was quite young — perseverance. Steadfastness. Staying power.

People seldom improve when they have no other model but themselves to copy after. — *Goldsmith*

Many times during my early months of radio work, I became so discouraged with how poorly I thought I was doing, I just wanted to throw in the towel — quit and go in another direction.

Jim in his wisdom sensed the despair in me. With each episode he would be determined not to allow me to give in and give up. He stirred within me an "I can" attitude that has continued to inspire me in every area of my life even to this day.

It was an inauspicious start, but I went on from that small station in Kansas to a reasonably successful career in broadcasting. Why? I believe it was because of Jim, my mentor. Thanks Jim!

Jim didn't just advise, but he took the time to help me improve my skills. As an effective mentor, he recognized the difference between advice and help.

He also believed in me and my abilities, and was quick to tell me so. But he didn't "coddle" or flatter his mentoree.

There is no future in any job.
The future lies in the attitude
of the person with the job.

Choosing a Professional Mentor

What characteristics should we look for in a mentor who can help us on the job?

Jean Driscoll, while speaking to a nursing conference, stated seven qualities we should be sensitive to if we're searching for a mentor. Although her address, "Rising to the Challenges of the '90s," was addressed to nurses and others in the field of medicine, her insights would be applicable to assisting anyone in choosing a mentor.

According to Jean Driscoll, these are the characteristics we should be looking for in a prospective mentor, particularly in a professional field:

1. An established practitioner
2. Highly motivated
3. Secure, healthy in self-concept
4. Accepting
5. Competent as a clinician/teacher
6. An expert in your specialty division
7. One who demonstrates leadership/professionalism

Ms. Driscoll goes on to say that these factors further the mentor to develop the conviction or belief that the protégé has potential. She adds that these seven characteristics of a mentor show they have the potential for commitment that is necessary for a productive relationship.

A positive mentoring experience has the potential of furthering your career. Your mentor will provide and assist in career planning, the management development, and the creativity that all businesses and organizations need and seek to recruit.

**The mentor can be the base-source of
your future success.**

Good and Bad Mentors

Rich DeVoss, a genius in network marketing, agrees that success in the corporate world rests in the mentoring relationship. In his book, *Compassionate Capitalism,* DeVoss states that we need to find someone whom we admire who has already achieved what we want to achieve and ask that person to help us reach our goals. That is the DeVoss definition of mentoring.

DeVoss shares certain mentoring philosophies that help us better understand the principles of mentoring in business. He includes the following:

- Mentors pass on to us knowledge that would be difficult for us to learn on our own.
- Mentors teach us the know-how to be successful in life.
- Mentors teach most who love best.
- Mentors have the courage to confront.
- Mentors make themselves available.

Mr. DeVoss points out that we need to beware of untrustworthy mentors. There are those who would try and take advantage of a guide-student program, DeVoss tells. He offers these guidelines in order to safeguard ourselves from such an experience:

- *The trustworthy mentor will not abuse your time.*

If you feel you're being pushed beyond your limits, watch out. The mentor who cares will always praise you for hard work, but will help you retain control over time commitments, etc.

• *A worthy mentor will not abuse your money.*

If your *"mentor"* starts wanting to control your money, heads up! The trustworthy mentor will help you with your finances, but will insist that you make your own final financial decisions.

• *A worthy mentor will not abuse discipline.*

He will build you up, not tear you down. The true mentor's goal is your independence, not for you to be dependent on them.

• *A worthy mentor will not abuse intimacy.*

He will not take advantage of your vulnerability. Moral and family values will be encouraged by the mentor of strong character.

• *A worthy mentor will not abuse authority.*

When the mentor tries to keep you under his thumb and expects unquestioning obedience to his every directive, be on the alert.

Mentoring should be a positive experience. When it ceases to be, because of extreme pressure being applied or unreasonable demands, the mentoree needs to seriously evaluate continuing.[1]

**For lack of training, they lacked
knowledge; for lack of knowledge,
they lacked confidence; and for lack
of confidence, they lacked victory.**
Julius Caesar

Nothing Magic About Losing

If you're a basketball fan (especially NBA) you know that Magic Johnson tried his hand as mentor of the Los Angeles Lakers for about 16 games. His coaching career was short-lived and the reason (according to Johnson) was the team's lack of pride.

Specifically, Johnson cited a lack of discipline and enthusiasm among the players. He couldn't understand why his players weren't bothered by losses.

Announcing his decision to step down as the Lakers coach, Magic said, "All I know is winning. That's all I want to know."

Something the Magic one hadn't considered when he agreed to take the team was their refusal to adapt themselves to the disciplines he expected of them — like being on time to practice or wearing jackets and ties on the road.

He said after spending even such a short time with the team he could see why they were where they were. The Lakers were eliminated from the play-off contention in April of 1994 — the first time in 17 years the team had not made it.

Mentors need to be able to look at major causes of failure and then deal with them. This is an important mentoring strategy. Mentors deal with techniques for prevention of failure as much as they deal with attitudes of achievement.

Job-Related Disciplines

After seeing the above article, I decided I would mentor my staff with the information I learned from Magic Johnson's dismal experience.

So with article in hand, I proceeded to communicate the need to take pride in ourselves by developing disciplines that would be reflected in our job performances.

In addition, I pointed out the following:

1. Losing should be a disappointing experience.

Not devastating — but disappointing.

A losing experience should disappoint us sufficiently for us to spend time analyzing what caused the loss. We should learn from the loss. If a salesperson loses a sale, they should re-play the presentation in their own mind so as to avert the same error again.

Athletic teams play game films the day after each game, win or lose, to analyze what can be done better.

2. Enthusiasm about who we are and what we do and why we do it is necessary for any degree of continued success.

Pride in our company, our product, and our position should instill enthusiasm. Enthusiasm is contagious; it's a self-propelling force that communicates confidence and conviction to all we come in contact with. Our customers will never be any more excited about us than we are about ourselves.

3. Teamwork comes first.

The major deficit in the Lakers approach to NBA Basketball was individual performance versus the need for teamwork. Coach Johnson said they had a lot of individual players who were just concerned about themselves, not the team.

4. Winning is not just an incident.

We have to study what we did right so we can prevent failure in the future.

I stressed to my staff that Johnson wanted "100 percent from the players every game." He also expected them to learn from every game — why they won or lost.

The Lakers are not champions because they refused to accept the basic rudiments in mentoring. They had everything going for them when Magic stepped in — except they didn't care.

Remember, even the mentor can't do magic, or, is it, the Magic couldn't do mentoring. Either way the results are the same.

Chapter Fifteen

Motivation and the Mentor

Mario Andretti, the great race car driver, said, "Desire is the key to motivation."

Motivation has also been defined as:

• What makes the difference between doing as little as you can get away with and doing everything you possibly can.

• The art of helping people to focus their minds and their energies on doing their work as effectively as possible.

• The art of creating conditions to which

the natural response of ordinary people is to accomplish extraordinary things.

The mentor motivates his mentoree to recognize his unaverage self and to accomplish the unaverage things in his life.

Desire is the key to motivation.

Authentic motivation is about making people productive. Real motivation is not designed to make people happy!

As a vice president and later president of nationwide sales and marketing organizations, I'm deeply aware of the need to know how to be more effective in motivating people.

As a consultant, I've had innumerable leaders and management people say to me, "I know Joe has great potential, but I just can't motivate him."

The motivator must develop a "need consciousness" toward the people to whom he is assigned. People respond when their "felt-needs" are addressed, not just their wants.

All too frequently we try to motivate by addressing extrinsic wants rather than directing motivation inwardly or intrinsically to the needs of the people.

I've spoken to thousands of network marketers here and abroad, and I always try to make this point: Don't use people to build your business; use your business to build people.

People are looking to the motivator to help them with their needs — whatever those needs might be. The mentor realizes that he must first see, and then encourage his mentoree to be a learner.

The student must be eager to learn. It frequently falls to the mentor, however, to assist in the development of that desire.

Ray Kroc of McDonalds says, "The french fry is my canvas, what's yours?"

Good question.

What is your canvas? To the mentor his protégé is his canvas. The mentor is aware of the rightness of his mentoree and then motivates him or her to be their "unaverage" self.

He also realizes that his mentoree must have a sense of expectancy when they encounter one another in a training session.

This is accomplished when the mentor provides his pupils with opportunities appropriate to his or her abilities and interests. Expectancy is stirred up when the platform of the partnering relationships contains the planks of an "I will, I can" attitude.

Don't underestimate the fact that application is what the session is about. The student learns then applies the wisdom or knowledge.

Robert Conray of Goldman, Sachs International, says, "Mentoring is a critical part of our company."

He adds, "most people come to our company right out of school, and they really learn the investment banking business by being put together with senior professionals."

The motivating coach of champions also equips

the student. In the marketplace a mentor is one who "adopts" a newcomer and provides tips on how to navigate the corporate waters.

The mentoring relationship is designed to help develop a good employee who has the appropriate training that produces knowledge that produces confidence. Confidence produces "championships" for everyone.

Encouragement is important, too. The marketplace mentor imparts to his students what that person needs in order to produce a rejuvenated attitude and heart.

The mentoree should emerge from every session revived, rejuvenated, and re-fired. There should be a positive change that takes place each time the mentor and the pupil get together.

The mentor motivates his mentorees to go a step beyond what they themselves, or others, might expect of them.

Vince Lombardi, coach of the Green Bay Packers, was perhaps the greatest mentor/motivator ever to step onto a football field.

I can remember being glued to a television set in 1966 watching the Lombardi-coached Packers pull out a come-from-behind 21-17 win over the Dallas Cowboys for the NFL championship.

What made the game so outstanding in my mind was the temperature and wind-chill in Wisconsin were at record lows, and the field was covered with a sheet of ice.

Yet, in those conditions, Green Bay put together a 65-yard drive that culminated with quarterback Bart Starr scoring from the one-yard line on the last play of the game.

The game, the attitude of the players, and the results reflected Lombardi's philosophy when he said, "Unless a man believes in himself and makes a total commitment to his career and puts everything he has into it — his mind, his body, and his heart — what is life worth to him? If I were a salesman, I would make this commitment to my company, the product, and most of all, to myself."

This creates a win-win situation for any company. That's why Motorola and ATT are just two of the "giants" who see the need for an effective "in-house" mentoring system.

The Spirit of Teamwork

A 1992 U.S. Small Business Administration report stated that nearly 62 percent of all businesses dissolve within the first six years.

Business analysts tell us one major cause of business failure rests in their inability to change. They refuse to keep pace with an ever-changing business environment and sociological trends.

TWA is one company making a tremendous effort at being open to change. Fighting the ill-effects of Chapter 11 bankruptcy, the employees of the company have taken over the ownership and management with great zeal and determination.

The force behind the resurgence of commitment and determination on the part of TWA staffers is rooted in good old-fashioned teamwork.

The old idea is simply put: Either we're pulling together or pulling apart. That's the spirit of teamwork.

Mentoring champions in the marketplace is oftentimes directed at the teamwork philosophy. Teamwork can be explained using T.E.A.M. as an acronym:

T = Together
E = Everyone
A = Achieves
M = More

The key word is "together." At TWA, employees from every facet of the company are coming "together" with the goal of serving their customers with greater efficiency.

The management "team" has formed what some have described as a powerful alliance dedicated to doing the job right the first time — from start to finish.

In part, the TWA mission statement supports the idea that "the customer is their reason for being." The goals and the emphasis of the employee is focused on making the mission statement happen.

In addition, the management team has established ambitious quality goals for the company and is providing the right conditions for employees to work together to achieve these goals.

A mentoring program in any business can help create that same kind of teamwork attitude. Knute Rockne put it this way:

The secret is to work less as individuals and more as a team. As a coach, I play not my eleven best, but my best eleven.

Now it's your chance, coach. You can mentor champions by molding them into a working unit. Find your best and mentor them into a team.

A Radical Approach?

Let's look at how one company initiated change in management concepts and adopted the basis for more effective teamwork at the same time.

Donnelly Corporation employs some 2,300 people with $232 million in sales annually. The company is held in high regard by their employees and customers alike, because they are constantly searching for ways to improve.

One program Donnelly has launched is called IDEAS, which stands for "Involved Donnelly Employees Achieve Success." The director of the program says the key to identifying needs and filling them is asking employees these ten questions:

1. What made you mad today?
2. What took too long?
3. What was the cause of any complaint?
4. What was misunderstood?
5. What costs too much?
6. What was wasted?
7. What was too complicated?
8. What was silly?
9. What job took too many people?
10. What job involved too many actions?

These questions are designed to help the employees think of problems and then solutions for those problems.

According to a company spokesperson, one-half of all Donnelly employees participate in the IDEAS program. With this kind of employee input, there's been a fresh attitude revealed among the people in the company.

The attitude? The company considers me important.

To some the IDEAS approach may seem radical. What we're suggesting is innovative thinking arranged around the mentoring method.

Seven Wisdom Principles

A business friend of mine has a procedure for mentoring new people when they come to work for his organization. The mentoring process always begins by giving these seven wisdom principles that will assist the new employee on how to conduct themselves on their new job.

He explains that every employer is looking for someone who will:

• *Give more of yourself than the company requires.*

In other words, be self-managed and readily adaptable to any changing situation the company might initiate.

• *Strive for excellence.*

The principle taught is simply this: For better or for worse, your work defines you.

• *Be self-motivated.*

For example, the successful employee should be the first to arrive and the last to leave. He is committed.

• *Don't criticize, condemn, or complain.*

The successful employee is loyal to the company, management, and other employees.

• *Pursue increased job knowledge and creativity.*

The motivated employee is involved in the company as an idea person.

• *Be enthusiastic.*

Zeal is an energy force that infects everyone in a positive fashion. Edward Butler had this to say: "One man has enthusiasm for 30 minutes, another for 30 days, but it's the man who has it for 30 years who makes a success in life."

• *Be group effective.*

In other words, be a team player. The motivated employee is adept at applying human relation skills in his relationships with others. He competes with no one but himself. He promotes, honors, and encourages the other team members.

These seven principles are simple, but my friend is reaping uncommon results. As he mentors these ideas into his employees, he is growing people who have the potential of taking his company to a new level of success.

Whether you are an employer or an employee, it's up to you to determine what values and behaviors are important — not only for your career goals but for you as a person. As a Christian, your main motivation should be to become more like Christ in all you say and do. If that is your objective, you will never fail at work — or in life.

Chapter Sixteen

Now It's
Your Turn

A few years ago while flying to a speaking engagement, I picked up an airline magazine and saw an article about Jon M. Huntsman, Chairman and CEO of the Huntsman Chemical Corporation.

Huntsman realizes that vision and an unconventional kind of creativity is required to make success happen. It's this kind of thinking that led Huntsman Chemical to come up with an innovation that changed the fast-food business — the "clam shell" hamburger container. Huntsman himself describes the sale of the McDonald container, "a marketing coup of sheer genius."

In that article about Jon Huntsman, I discovered several key principles that pointed to his success. As we examine these strategies, they should encourage us to mentor these concepts into the life of others and, at the same time, allow these ideas to be released in our own lives.

Strategy One: Take control of your circumstances.

Huntsman chose the geographical location for his plant based on the fact he personally wanted to centralize the three important focuses of his life: his family, his business, and his volunteer church work.

Strategy Two: Stay focused and make wise decisions.

Jon Huntsman is focused on whatever demands his attention and at the same time is able to make decisions with great confidence.

Mentor your protégé in the area of a single-focused approach to problem-solving and train them to make decisions with confidence.

Strategy Three: Surround yourself with positive, creative people.

Huntsman credits much of his past successes with the fact that he surrounds himself with bright young men and women "who don't know it can't be done."

Strategy Four: Use the past for your advantage.

Where we came from or the adversity of our past is not a reason for failing to achieve our dream. Huntsman believes that past negative circumstances can be "great incentives" to developing the attitude that adversity can be turned toward the positive.

Strategy Five: Keep your promises, and do what you say you will do.

"Teach the philosophy that your handshake is your bond," says Huntsman. He believes that once even verbal agreement has been reached, there is no turning back. He will not compromise his integrity. That's the bottom-line issue of character.

Strategy Six: Make the most out of every opportunity.

Don't do anything half-heartedly. Mr. Huntsman points out, however, that balance is required in all of life: "Never take it so seriously that you're unable to have fun."

Strategy Seven: Be a person with vision.

As an entrepreneur himself, Huntsman's credo states that only a person with vision can be a good entrepreneur. A good entrepreneur must also be a "risktaker" and a good "gamesman" who is able to keep his challenger a little off balance.[1]

Jon Huntsman's philosophy of business and life should be an inspiration to all of us. Although I've not had the privilege of meeting him personally, Jon will always be remembered by me as the "father" of the Big Mac containers.

Never Too Old

Ethel doesn't like to talk about age — although she acknowledges being more than 80 years old.

What Ethel Krupsky does like to talk about is her sales career with World Book Encyclopedias, which began in 1957. Over 30 years later she still lugs books and contracts to homes, schools, and businesses.

Ethel holds the World Book record for selling 100 orders a year for 35 years! She also has more than five years logged in her company's heralded Two-Hundred-Orders-A-Year Club.

Can you imagine having the privilege of being mentored by such a champion as Ethel Krupsky?

In studying her approach to her career, we learn these simple but time-proven concepts that this mighty octogenarian can teach us:

Concept One: Age is no hindrance.

As someone has said: "I don't feel old. I feel like a young person who has learned something."

Concept Two: Age is an asset.

Ethel uses what some would see as a liability to her advantage.

Concept Three: Pursue excellence.

Nothing average satisfies Ethel. She pursues excellence even after many years of proven achievement.

Concept Four: Be self-motivated.

"Helping children" is what motivates Ethel to make "at least one more call." She is self-motivated.

Concept Five: Maintain a high energy level.

"I'm too busy to get tired," Ethel notes. Even as an octogenarian she has positive energy that keeps her re-fired.

Concept Six: Work hard and keep your commitments.

The ex-school "marm's" old-fashioned work ethic has produced the success she has experienced. Hard work, faithfulness, and commitment make up her philosophy of work.

Concept Seven: Love your work.

She says of her job, "This has been a most enjoyable career." Successful people love their work.

I stand in awe of people like Ethel who teach us that age should never be an excuse for not pursuing excellence and striving to reach our goals.

Ramon Blanco Suarez, a Venezuelan guitar maker, was the oldest person to climb the 29,000-foot Mt. Everest. But then, he was only 60!

Only goes to prove you're never too old to pursue your dream!

Do Unto Others

In 1993, 8.7 million batteries were sold by 345 independent dealerships serving over 200,000 retail outlets throughout North America. The company? Interstate Battery Systems, Inc. of Dallas, Texas, now the undisputed champion in the automobile battery business.

What is the reason for this company's phenomenal growth? The leadership philosophies of CEO Norm Miller.

In a recent interview on television, Mr. Miller told his fascinating story and shared some of his innovative business ideas.

Interstate's impressive corporate headquarters include the usual maps showing the company's marketing system and samples of IB's batteries. In the middle of their accounting and marketing departments, however, is a chaplain's office.

The IB staff includes a full-time chaplain who is available to help meet the personal needs of the employees. He also handles the contributions that Interstate makes to missions and missionaries and their families.

In another part of the corporate complex is the corporate library, which is stocked with Christian tapes and books! Norm Miller is no ordinary CEO.

Perhaps the most unique aspect of Interstate Batteries is the goal or philosophy that keeps the organization focused. Mr. Miller puts it this way: "Our goal is simply 'Do unto others.' We feel it's simply the best business philosophy we could have."

This unusual CEO goes on to say this about keeping his customers happy: "If I look out for your needs and how I can meet them, and then try in my heart to do it, I'll come closer to accomplishing my goal."

This concept of doing business, however, was not always the way Norm Miller believed.

A Winning Attitude

Although he had always been "successful" and had reached every goal he ever set, Miller said his life at one point was unfulfilled and empty. The "things and the deals" left him realizing there had to be more to life than mere "stuff."

After an all-night drinking binge, Norm realized

he was a white-collar alcoholic, headed downhill on a fast track. One morning it dawned on him that he had lost control of his life, just as his alcoholic father had done.

So Norm started seeking the truth. He wanted to find out if God was real. He joined a Bible study group and began his search. In the process, he says, he gave the Bible study leader a real challenge!

When he had gathered enough evidence to prove to himself that God was real, he found a mentor who nurtured him in his new-found faith.

Speaking of his spiritual experience, Norm puts it this way: "By the time I bought Interstate Batteries in 1978, my relationship with Christ was so much a part of my life, it was only natural to bring God right into the board room."

Norm is as tenacious as any person you'd ever want to meet. Although he is a "nice man," make no mistake, he's no pushover at the negotiating table, where he has been said to get a nickel out of every penny. He doesn't like to lose, and his competitive attitude guides him at the office and also on the race track.

Norm experiences life now at its fullest. Whether it's taking part in the Interstate Battery-sponsored Great American Vintage Car Race, or joining buddy Joe Gibbs to watch the Interstate Battery car win in the Daytona 500, Norm loves to play the game almost as much as he loves winning.

Oh, by the way, Norm is now mentoring many others in the ways of business and in the ways of life.

How About You?

As you've read this book, you have probably remembered all the people who have mentored you over the years. Now, you think, you'd like to give to others some of what you have learned.

Who could gain the most from what you have to offer? Do you have skills and experience that could benefit someone less experienced and in need of on-the-job training? Or maybe you know people who are lacking the character traits they need to succeed in life.

Whatever your area of expertise, I know you have something to offer someone else. All you have to do is look for the opportunity! Now it's your turn.

Notes

Chapter Two
[1]Nelson Annan, "Square Bamboo," *The Christian Reader,* March/April 1993. Used with permission.

Chapter Three
[1]Norman Schwartzkopf, *It Doesn't Take a Hero* (New York, NY: Bantam Books Division of Doubleday-Dell).

Chapter Four
[1]*Leadership* magazine, June 7, 1994.
[2]Peggy Anderson, *Great Quotes from Great Women* (Lombard, IL: Celebrating Excellence Publishing Co.).

Chapter Seven
[1]Margaret Jensen.
[2]Family Research Council, 700 13th Street, NW, Suite 500, Washington, DC 20005.
[3]Chuck Colson and Jack Eckerd, *Why America Doesn't Work* (Dallas, TX: Word Publishing, 1991).

Chapter Eight
[1]*Pastors Update,* February 1993, Fuller Evangelistic Assoc.

Chapter Eleven
[1]Richard Nixon, *Leaders* (Beaverton, OR: Simon & Schuster/Touchstone).
[2]Terrie Pergason, *Designed to Disciple: The Mentor's Role in Developing Leadership* (Charles E. Fuller Institute, 1993).

Chapter Twelve
[1]Joseph Gosse, *Unemployed Workers*, part of a series of publications on "The Spirituality of Work," developed by the National Center for the Laity, Chicago, IL.
[2]Colson and Eckerd, *Why America Doesn't Work.*
[3]Colson and Eckerd, *Why America Doesn't Work.*

Chapter Fourteen
[1]Rich DeVoss, *Compassionate Capitalism* (New York, NY: Dutton, Div. of Penguin Books USA, 1993).

Chapter Sixteen
[1]*Sky* magazine, July 1989.